NOTHING NEW UNDER THE SUN

a cosmic timeline for earth

Sean Kayvon Sedghi

SATURN USA

Copyright © 2020 Saturn USA

All rights reserved

ISBN: 9798722892874

Library of Congress Control Number: 2018675309
Printed in the United States of America

CONTENTS

Title Page
Copyright
01 Intro — 1
02 Ancient World History — 6
03 Classics — 14
04 Democracy — 25
05 Republic — 30
06 Middle Ages — 38
07 Renaissance — 44
08 Scientific Revolution — 52
09 Enlightenment — 58
10 United States of America — 66
11 Age of Aquarius — 74
12 End of Time — 86
About The Author — 95

01 Intro
Philosophy—Wisdom—History—Religion
Classical Education—Modern Education—STEM

02 Ancient World History
Cosmic Time—Levels of Creation
Basic History of Earth—Greek Mythology
Golden Age—Titans vs Olympians
Silver Age—Bronze Age—Heroic Age—Iron Age
Economics—Structure vs Expression—Jupiter

03 Classics
Western Philosophy—Paganism—Judaism
Mythical vs Intellectual—Humanities
Liberal Arts—Golden Age of Greece
Socrates—Trial of Socrates—Plato
Theory of Forms—Aristotle—Virtue Ethics

04 Democracy
Political Science—Aristotle's Politics
Growth—Power Elite—Emotion vs Logic
Public Education—Leadership

05 Republic
Democracy vs. Republic—Public Entity—Aristocracy
Plato's Republic—Gold—Silver—Bronze
Free Time—Strengths/Weaknesses

06 Middle Ages
Greece to Rome—Catholic Church
East-West Schism—Catholic Europe
Dark Ages—Feudalism—Black Death

07 Renaissance
Taxes —More Books—Inquisition—Italian Renaissance—Florence
Divine Comedy—Northern Renaissance—Protestant Reformation
Universe Cities—Early Modern Literature—Shakespeare

08 Scientific Revolution
Deductive vs. Inductive—Aristotle's Organon

Medieval Scholasticism—Research Universities Novum
Organum—Scientific Materialism
Natural Philosophy—Natural Science

09 Enlightenment
Diversity—Freethinking—Globalization—Liberty
Russian Enlightenment—Dutch—German—French—English

10 United States of America
Great Awakening—Founding Fathers
British America—French America
Federalist Party—Anti-Federalist Party
Articles of Confederation—U.S. Constitution
Strict vs. Loose Interpretation—Trailblazer for Freedom

11 Age of Aquarius
Greek Words for Time—Astronomy—Logos
Astrology—Saturn and Uranus—Water-Bearer Air Waves—Freedom vs.
Tradition Avant-Garde USA in Aquarius—Aquarian Technology
Aquarian Business Models—Pisces to Aquarius

12 End of Time
Time Bubble—End of Chronos—Chronic Disease
Crystallization —Light Quotient—Universal Library
Eschatology—Free Will Planet—Age of Capricorn

01 INTRO

Before studying history, it's helpful to gain an understanding of something that transcends time altogether—philosophy.

Philosophy

Philosophy is basically synonymous with wisdom. The word philosophy comes from the Greek word philosophia meaning "love of wisdom".

o   philo- (love, friendship)
o   sophia (wisdom)

Ultimately, you can't capture philosophy with a definition. You can describe it in many ways, but you can't put philosophy in a box.

"What is wisdom?"

Trying to define philosophy is like trying to define wisdom. It's an abstract concept that everyone has their own idea of. But that certainly doesn't make wisdom any less valuable.

Wisdom

The concept of Wisdom is personified as a feminine being in various mythologies across world history.

Chokhmah (Wisdom) serves as a central concept in Hebrew culture. According to the Book of Proverbs, Wisdom is the primordial spirit which was at God's side while he was crafting our universe.

From a material perspective, wisdom is the key variable between a heavenly world and a hellish world. When civilizations choose to cultivate a positive relationship with wisdom, peace and abundance manifest. When civilizations disregard wisdom, chaos manifests.

The goal of studying philosophy is to eliminate suffering by enriching your consciousness with wisdom.

This is an infinite process where you are continuously transcending yourself. You often hear people describe the "pursuit of wisdom" and philosophy is exactly that—an endless pursuit.

Under the right circumstances, you can reach a point where you virtually eliminate suffering from your personal life. However, if you work to help reduce collective suffering, then you always have more room to grow.

With proper appreciation for philosophy, you can directly manifest your desires onto the physical plane. In other words, studying philosophy allows you to turn your dreams into reality. On the flip side, a disrespect for the universal principles of philosophy will inevitably flood your life with stress.

History

In this book, history is framed according to the willingness of the planet to embrace philosophy over time.

This willingness is a variable that is abstract and not directly measurable. However, you can clearly determine the willingness of a particular civilization to embrace philosophy by observing the degree of suffering they experience over time.

With philosophy, civilizations prosper. Without philosophy, they self-destruct. Wisdom is the difference between joy and misery.

When you look at the history of the planet, it's obvious that suffering has been the norm for a long time. That lets you know that historically most of our civilizations have been lacking in philosophical understanding.

Religion

Religions have been central to Western history (to say the least). However, when discussing history over cosmic time frames, it's more practical to describe the role of philosophy in human affairs than religion.

This is because philosophy is a more general term that applies to any period of history. A civilization always has a relationship with philosophy, but a civilization doesn't always have a relationship with religion.

Philosophy is a broader term that spans across all cultures, over all periods of time. Philosophy existed before the creation of our world.

Religion is a more precise term that describes specific belief systems which were given to humanity through divine revelations at specific points in time.

Ultimately, the two are both geared towards the same goal: enlightenment.

Classical Education

For most of Western history, education = philosophy!

There were still distinct educational disciplines, but they all fell under the umbrella of philosophy. For example—mathematics, geometry, mythology, logic, etc. are all just different types of philosophical pursuits. The knowledge contained in each of these disciplines can help you reduce suffering if integrated into your life properly.

The ancient Greek and Roman cultures are generally referred to as the basis for all of Western culture, and therefore Greek and Roman cultures are referred to as "classical".

The entire Greek and Roman educational systems was based around philosophy. In other words, the entire classical education system was focused on teaching wisdom to the youth.

Modern Education

In theory, our modern educational system should be centered on philosophy, considering that we are building upon the classical foundation. However, an objective look at the modern Western public education system will tell you that is not always this case.

At elite institutions, a well-rounded education always includes an emphasis on philosophy. But at most public schools, philosophy is not a primary focus.

Philosophy was never supposed to be superseded in educational priority by anything! What is more important than wisdom? But somehow philosophy has slipped out of focus in many of our educational systems on earth.

Surely this has been a tragedy, but reintegrating philosophy into our public educational system in the modern age is complicated. Essentially what has happened over the past few centuries is that philosophy has been replaced by materialistic science. This has undoubtedly served a purpose, but the unbalanced focus on science (instead of philosophy) that exists in modern education is counter-productive and is actually one of the greatest hindrances to the spiritual growth of earth as a whole.

STEM

Modern science has undeniably helped civilizations progress, but to have students pass through an educational system—especially through a university—without really studying philosophy is just tragic.

STEM (Science, Technology, Engineering, Mathematics) is an acronym used to refer to the fields of learning in modern Western education that make a very strict use of the scientific method. Basically, modern STEM disciplines are taught within a paradigm that disregards the existence of an immaterial reality. STEM curriculums are designed to give the student straightforward, practical skills to contribute to society in a measurable fashion.

There is nothing wrong with science, technology, engineering, and mathematics as academic disciplines. The way they are taught in modern Western education is problematic, but the disciplines themselves are not.

STEM education is a good thing, but only when balanced with a well-rounded liberal arts education. An education void of philosophy, i.e. a purely STEM education, is counterproductive to spiritual growth.

It does you little good to acquire STEM knowledge if you don't first have knowledge of how to eliminate suffering from your experience. In other words, it's difficult to make a healthy contribution to society if your experience of life is flooded with stress due to a lack of wisdom.

02 ANCIENT WORLD HISTORY

As mentioned last chapter, we can describe world history within a relatively simple framework based on mankind's willingness to embrace philosophy over time.

It's useful to explore the concept of time on a cosmic scale, so that we can properly contextualize the current cycle of creation on earth. In other words, it helps to look at history from a cosmic perspective before zooming in to an earthly perspective.

<u>Cosmic Time</u>

First of all, cosmic time is infinite and exists independently of our planet.

Cosmic time is an infinite linear line. I couldn't tell you where it begins or ends, but that's not very to us here on earth. More importantly, that infinite linear line includes individual circular pockets of time, or cycles of creation.

The construct of time that exists on our planet is indeed one of these circular pockets of time. Generally speaking, the people who live within a cycle of creation are unaware of the infinite cosmic timeline. In terms of modern society, many people don't think creation exists outside of the physical universe.

<u>Levels of Creation</u>

Within spiritual systems of thought, it's accepted that there are many, many levels of creation. Our planet is merely one level of creation.

I don't say that to diminish the importance of life on our planet. Rather, I say that because once you learn to see our planet from a cosmic perspective, the history of life on earth becomes much simpler. It cuts away all of the emotional ties from your perception and allows you to gain an understanding of history that is clear, simple, and most importantly—accurate.

You have two basic types of planets:

-The first type of planet is characterized by complete cooperation of the inhabitants and the experience of life on these planets is heavenly. Suffering is virtually nonexistent. The people are in tune with the infinite cosmic timeline.

-The second type of planet is characterized by inhabitants who are still learning to cooperate with each other on a collective level. On these planets, suffering is the default state of being and the people are generally not aware of higher levels of creation.

Basic History of Our Planet

The Fall of Man describes the decent of mankind from a perfect state of consciousness into a lower state of consciousness. When this process took place, our current circular cycle of creation was generated.

In other words, the civilizations of earth originally existed in a state of perfection. Our planet was in harmony with the infinite cosmic timeline. The dreams and desires of the people manifested directly into the physical plane without resistance from the universe because philosophy was fully embraced by the citizens.

Over time, mankind lost touch with the original ancient wisdom and descended into a lower state of collective consciousness. As a consequence, the civilizations on earth began to suffer. This state of suffering is one of the underlying characteristics of our entire cycle of creation.

Greek Mythology

I'm going to describe the history of our planet using the basic structure provided by the Greek philosopher Hesiod. The works of Hesiod form the basis of Greek mythology and include the popular

Greek gods that many people are familiar with.

In his classical poem Works and Days, Hesiod discusses the creation of our planet and how we have ended up in our current situation on earth. The poem given by Hesiod was echoed centuries later in Rome by the poet Ovid in his major work Metamorphoses (Latin for "transformations").

For the most part, Ovid's Roman mythology is identical to Hesiod's Greek mythology, and therefore I won't discuss Ovid's any further. I will, however, use the Roman names for the planets instead of the Greek names.

Golden Age of Saturn

The Golden Age of Saturn was the first period of time on our planet, ruled by the first generation of beings who embodied on earth—the Titans. The Titans are a playful group of beings who are led by their youngest member, Saturn. Saturn holds an adamantine sickle given to him by Mother Earth and is known as the god of agriculture.

The Golden Age was a period of time in which the people lived in perfect harmony with nature. The people lived as gods, and they lived among the gods. The earth naturally produced an abundance of fruit and the people channeled all of their energy towards creative pursuits. The people easily communicated with the animals on earth and there was certainly no need to slaughter them for food!

In the Golden Age, the people lived happily for long periods of time and they passed away peacefully, as if they were merely falling asleep. These souls lived on in the afterlife as benevolent guardians for earth called daimons in Greek.

The Golden generation was illiterate because there was no need for written manuscripts. In addition, there was no boats because the Golden generation did not travel across the globe. They had plenty of natural resources available in their homelands and they had no desire to travel for leisure.

There was no need for external laws or government as everything was in divine order. This does not mean that there was a lack of justice for actions that were less than perfect. The system of justice is built into the fabric of our material reality. The citizens of the Golden Age were fully aware of this, and therefore the people freely chose to respect the laws of nature because they knew it was in their own enlightened self-interest to do so.

Titans vs. Olympians

In Greek mythology, the transition between the Golden Age and the Silver Age was the consequence of an event known as the Titanomachy (Greek for "Titan Battle"). The Titanomachy was a battle for the rulership of our universe between the Titans (led by Saturn) and the Olympians (led by Jupiter).

NOTE: The depiction of the Titans in the Disney movie "Hercules" is unfair and inaccurate!

Again, our universe was originally led by the Titans. The Titanomachy marks the shift where the majority of people on earth chose to follow the Olympians in favor of the Titans. With the help of the Hundred-Handers and the Cyclopes, the Olympians defeated the Titans after a ten-year battle.

Since that point, our universe has been ruled by the Olympians. The responsibilities for rulership were divided among the Olympians, primarily Jupiter, Neptune, and Pluto. The Titans were imprisoned in a gloomy abyss known as Tartarus.

Silver Age

It's ironic that we glorify the imprisonment of the Titans considering that this imprisonment is precisely the development that transitioned the planet OUT of the Golden Age and down into the Silver Age! Hesiod and Ovid both tell us very clearly that the Golden Age was superior in every way relative to the Silver Age.

Nevertheless, the people wanted to send the Titans to Tartarus and so it happened.

The descent into the Silver Age marks the point where Jupiter created the four-seasons (spring, summer, autumn, winter). Life on earth during the Golden Age consisted of an eternal springtime with an abundance of fruits that grew naturally. In the

Silver Age, the people were required to plant seeds for agriculture and to build shelters for protection from harsh weather.

The people lived like children with their mothers for one-hundred years before becoming adults. However, once they became adults they quickly began to self-destruct by way of foolishness. There was no widespread war or conflict during this period, but the people did grow increasingly disagreeable towards each other.

Bronze Age

After a period of time, Jupiter grew impatient with the Silver generation and destroyed them with a thunderbolt.

With the transition from the Silver Age to the Bronze Age, life on earth decayed into more miserable conditions. The biggest difference between the Silver generation and the Bronze generation is that the Bronze generation loved war and conflict.

Whereas the Silver generation had disagreements with each other, the Bronze generation took their disagreements to the extreme and engaged in full-blown wars. The people in the Bronze Age still honored the gods, but they also used the gods in vain as justification for war and destruction. Furthermore, the people began to develop a strong sense of pride based on achievements in war.

According to Hesiod, the Bronze race loved "the lamentable works of Mars (god of war)". So, the Golden Age is associated with Saturn, the Silver Age with Jupiter, and the Bronze Age with Mars.

There was no more justice on earth during the Bronze A ge as people arbitrarily killed each other as a consequence of erroneous beliefs. In other words, spirituality in the Bronze Age had become severely fractured and people began to justify wars based on a narrow-minded understanding of reality.

Heroic Age

The Heroic Age is characterized by heroes who spoke out against the detestable acts of war committed during the Bronze Age. That's not to say war is always unavoidable, but rather that a civilization should not inherently love war.

The Heroic Age was somewhat of a bubble within the Bronze Age. The existence of the Heroic Age was the result of the positive choices made by the individual heroes on earth as a reaction to the negative Bronze Age culture. Jupiter created the Bronze Age and the Iron Age, but Jupiter did not create the Heroic Age.

The heroes were considered to be superhuman or demigods, but not divine beings. Tragically, the Heroic Age was short-lived as the heroes died in war.

On the bright side, the heroes were granted access to special region in the heavens known as Elysium (also known as the Elysian Fields and the Islands of the Blessed) in their afterlife. Elysium is an exclusive location where the Titans reside in the heavens and it is beyond reach for most beings from earth.

With the heroes gone to Elysium, many of the best leaders were departed from earth. As that happened, earth gradually descended back to the Bronze Age.

Iron Age

The Iron Age began when Jupiter grew impatient with the Bronze generation and destroyed them with a thunderbolt.

The Iron Age is basically the complete opposite of the Golden Age. Hesiod describes life in the Iron Age as, "labor and sorrow by day, perishing by night". The people age very rapidly in the Iron Age compared to the previous ages.

Whereas in the Golden Age the people didn't have to work, in the Iron Age the people are forced to work (sometimes in slavery). This dynamic where the people are forced into labor was not in the original blueprint for our planet. However, the forced labor became necessary over time as the people continuously refused to accept accountability for their own actions.

Piety is completely gone from civilization in the Iron Age. The people hate each other and tell lies shamelessly. Men wait for their wives to die and women wait for their husbands to die. Children dishonor their parents and everyone acts in their own self-interest. In addition, people dig up natural resources (gold, silver, gemstones, fossil fuels) from inside the earth and hoard them for commercialization during the Iron Age.

Economics

By definition, economics describes the distribution of resources under scarcity.

Economics didn't exist during the Golden Age because scarcity didn't manifest on the physical plane during the Golden Age. There was no economics because the earth produced all of the necessary resources in abundance.

That's not to say there was an infinite amount of physical resources during the Golden Age. Our planet exists as a finite reality, and so there will always be a finite amount of physical resources.

However, the people in the Golden Age clearly understood that the planet, under the right circumstances, can easily produce an abundance of resources for the needs of all people (food, water, shelter). The modern economic notion that we simply don't have enough resources to survive is completely out of touch with Golden Age ideals.

In short, there was no economics in the Golden Age because the Golden generation had no concept of scarcity. Scarcity is not normal and it is not a fundamental part of our reality.

Structure vs. Expression

There is a particular structure to our material universe and, within that structure, we can experience a very broad range of material expressions.

The planet went from the expression of playfulness (Golden Age) to the expression of misery (Iron Age). It's important to consider that the structure of the material universe never fundamentally changed over the progression of the ages on our planet. The expression of the material universe certainly did shift, but only as a result of the choices mankind made on a collective level.

The only variable that changed between the Golden Age and the Iron Age is the collective consciousness of the people on earth, more specifically mankind's willingness to embrace philosophy.

The underlying structure of the universe did not change.

Resource scarcity is a particular expression of our material universe, and it has been created as a consequence of collective state of consciousness shared by the people on earth. However, scarcity is not a part of the structure of our material universe.

Jupiter

It's definitely not the fault of Jupiter, or any other individual leader, that mankind fell out of the Golden Age. The fall from the Golden Age was a consequence of the choices made by mankind on a collective level.

Jupiter did everything he could to prevent mankind from continuing to slip downwards in consciousness. However, people make their choices independently of Jupiter and he fully respects the free will of individuals. Therefore, Jupiter never tried to force the citizens of earth to learn about the laws of nature. He definitely encouraged it, but he knew it would be futile to attempt to force the people to learn anything.

03 CLASSICS

The time period from ancient Greece to ancient Rome is termed classical antiquity. The study of classical antiquity is referred to simply as Classics, and it is a foundational part of modern Western education.

Classics is an essential element of Western education because Greece and Rome are looked upon as examples of enlightened societies and cultural perfection.

Western Philosophy

We shouldn't say that philosophy as a whole originated in Greece, but rather that Western philosophy originated in Greece. The specific term "philosophy" did technically originate in Greece, but the concept of divine wisdom (sophia) goes back much further.

In particular, Western philosophy is concerned with deriving wisdom from the power of the human intellect. In other words, Western philosophers generally seek to find rational solutions to their problems by using careful logic.

This sort of intellectualism is not the only path to wisdom, as other cultures prefer to take more spiritual or intuitive approaches to solve their problems.

Paganism

The word pagan is an umbrella term used to describe all of the belief systems that existed before the major monotheistic religions (Judaism, Christianity, Islam). Of course, paganism includes an extremely broad set of belief systems.

Historically speaking, you could say that the pagan world was very chaotic in terms of philosophical practices. It's important we do not label all pagan practices as unacceptable, but civility was oftentimes absent in the ancient pagan world due to a lack of unity among the people.

With such a vast—and loosely defined—array of pagan belief systems, it became common for people to engage in violent behavior with the idea in mind that they were performing some proper ritual. Poor intercultural understanding and over-aggression also resulted in plenty of brutish conflicts among pagan tribes.

Nonetheless, there were (and still are) many interesting pagan systems on earth. Most of them included the worship nature in some form. For example, many people worshipped the Sun as the giver of life. Other pagans might have worshipped a number of demi-gods or even worshipped nature as an impersonal entity.

Mythology is a precise term that describes specific pagan systems, usually including legends describing a how a pantheon of supernatural beings formulated our reality. You can basically use the words myth and mythology interchangeably, although myth is a more generic term. Mythology specifically refers to myths concerning the divine plan for our universe, whereas myths can be any sort of story passed down through word-of-mouth.

Judaism

Judaism is one of the most fascinating and unique topics to study in world history.

You could definitely say that Judaism, as opposed to Greek philosophy, is the foundation for Western culture. It really just depends if you're focused on the development of Western secular culture or Western religious culture.

Judaism is widely considered to be the world's first major monotheistic religion, and it emerged out of a pagan environment.

Although it's considered a "major" religion, the Jews have always been a minority on the world stage. Jewish culture was surely alive and well in Ancient Greece, but the Jews never grew in number like the Christians and Muslims have done, for a number of reasons.

However, the positive impact of Judaism across all of Western history far outweighs what you would expect, based on the number of Jews proportional to the total Western population. It's really quite the mystery.

In contrast to pagan systems of belief, Judaism proposes the existence of one true God. This idea of monotheism makes Judaism more structured than pagan systems. In addition, Jewish culture is characterized by a strong sense of spiritual unity among the people—a unity which did not exist in polytheistic cultures.

Although monotheism was a unique feature for Judaism, Jewish culture still has much in common with pagan culture. In particular, myths and symbols are foundational elements within both Jewish and pagan cultures.

Mythical vs. Intellectual

Mythical teachings use symbols to communicate wisdom, and they are primarily designed to expand the consciousness of the learner.

You can contrast mythical consciousness with intellectual consciousness, which has increasingly become the dominant mode of consciousness in the West. With an intellectual teaching you are trying to communicate the specific details of a given situation, in order to provide straightforward information to the learner.

When an individual activates his or her intellect, they are accessing all of the information that already exists within their mind. They use their intellect to examine a given stimuli, comparing it to all of their pre-existing knowledge. Therefore, the individual's ability to intellectually analyze a situation is completely dependent on his or her pre-existing knowledge.

The major limitation with teaching through the intellectual mind is that it's difficult to for a teacher to communicate new and abstract teachings to the student in a timely manner. In other words, it's difficult to teach a student about unfamiliar, abstract concepts by using intellectual communication because the student has no frame of reference to build from. The student must undergo a lengthy learning process where they become familiarized with foundational concepts so that they may later learn about the same subject in a more advanced fashion.

This is especially true when the concepts being learned are spiritual in nature, because spiritual reality can often be totally unfamiliar to a person who is entangled in their material experience on earth. Therefore, mythical teachings are a suitable way to introduce spiritual concepts to people who are not yet prepared to understand them on an intellectual level.

Ancient myths were never meant to be taken literally, and the educated people who lived in the ancient world never dreamed of doing so!

Humanities

Greek philosophy champions the use of the human intellect to solve worldly problems. This tradition of studying life through the power of the human intellect alone developed into a field of study known as the humanities.

The term humanities was originally used in contrast to divinity, or receiving knowledge from divine revelation. The humanities were a groundbreaking development because they provided a way for humans to grow their understanding of nature through their own efforts. For all of history before the humanities, people relied on either divine revelation or external authority figures for guidance.

In modern education, humanities is often used to contrast with science (scientific materialism). This is because the humanities seek solutions to worldly problems by using the human intellect and scientific materialism seeks solutions by collecting scientific data through very strict experiments.

Liberal Arts

Another central component of Western education which came from Greece is the seven liberal arts.

The liberal arts are skills which every person who is pursuing freedom on earth should master. In other words, the liberal arts are the skills that an educated person must have in order to contribute genuine value to society without physical labor.

Without mastery of the seven liberal arts, an individual will be unable to sustainably accumulate independent wealth. In order to survive, such an individual will be inevitably forced into some sort of physical labor (often agriculture), thereby squandering their freedom.

Mastering the liberal arts, in contrast to philosophy, is not supposed to be a lifelong pursuit. Whereas the individual is continuously seeking higher forms of wisdom with philosophy, the liberal arts are supposed to be mastered within a relatively short period of time.

One way to think of the liberal arts is that they are a common language which is shared by all people on earth. The liberal arts provide a way for us all to communicate and, ultimately, cooperate with each other.

Below I have listed the seven liberal arts. The first three liberal arts (trivium) are considered to be a prerequisite for learning the final four liberal arts (quadrivium).

NOTE: This model of the liberal arts was created in the Middle Ages. The liberal arts were not as clearly defined in ancient Greece, and therefore the Middle Age model is easier to understand.

Trivium (Latin for "place where three roads meet")
- 1) Grammar – proper language use
- 2) Logic – clear thinking
- 3) Rhetoric – communication and leadership

Quadrivium ("place where four roads meet")
- 4) Arithmetic –numbers and quantity
- 5) Geometry – relationships between variables
- 6) Cosmology – heavenly bodies
- 7) Music – harmonics between heaven and earth

Golden Age of Greece

Socrates, Plato, and Aristotle are three of the most influential philosophers in the history of Western civilization. The period in which they lived is known as Classical Greece, and it is considered to be the Golden Age of Greek civilization. During the classical period, Athens was the philosophical center of the world.

These three men taught philosophy to Athenians in a chain of succession, with Socrates mentoring Plato and Plato mentoring Aristotle. We shouldn't say that Socrates, Plato, and Aristotle were the only philosophers in ancient Greece, but their legacy surely stands above the rest.

It's tough to generalize the thoughts of these three men because the scope of their works is so incredibly broad. They applied their intellect to just about every area of human life. In short, they sparked the flame of Western philosophy through their works.

Socrates

Socrates was a thoughtful individual who was the subject of much controversy in ancient Greece. This man acquired a vast amount of knowledge over the course of his life, and he wasn't shy about sharing it. A popular image of Socrates is that of an old man in the Athenian public forum arguing passionately with other citizens about various philosophical topics.

A system of discourse known as the Socratic method, where the two parties ask each other questions to provoke critical thinking and illuminate subconscious thought patterns, is a key component of Western philosophy (and Western law).

Mostly everything we know about Socrates comes from his characterization in Plato's works. Socrates never actually published anything himself, which is surprising considering how popular he is.

It's unclear to what extent Socrates actually held the beliefs expressed in Plato's works, as opposed to Socrates's character merely serving as a proxy for Plato to share his own beliefs. Regardless, Socrates is personally credited for providing much of the foundation of Western philosophy through Plato's texts.

Trial of Socrates

Many people in ancient Greece believed Socrates was harming children/teenagers by teaching them philosophy before they were old enough to think independently.

His accusers believed that Socrates was disrupting the natural development of the youth by teaching them philosophical concepts which contradicted socially accepted norms. In other words, Socrates was accused of introducing philosophical concepts that were too complex for children to properly understand.

With a partial, but insufficient, understanding of philosophy, the youth began to behave immorally and rebel against social norms. The youth would attempt to justify their immoral behavior by using fallacious arguments based on their limited understanding of philosophy, which had been supplied by Socrates. Therefore, Socrates was accused of corrupting the youth.

Whether Socrates was actually crossing the line with his actions, or whether he was merely a scapegoat, is up for debate.

Nonetheless, Greece was a democracy at the time, and so the judgement of Socrates was carried out by a democratic jury. Socrates was a very self-assured—bordering on arrogant—man and therefore he refused to apologize to the Athenians because he did not believe he had committed a crime. As a result, Socrates was convicted by the Athenians with the charges of corrupting the youth.

In addition, Socrates was charged with insubordination to the will of the Greek gods. Socrates said he communicated with a daimonion (Greek for "divine thing) throughout his life. According to Socrates, the daimonion would warn him against making mistakes, but didn't affect his life otherwise.

Socrates elevated his personal supernatural experiences above commonly-held Greek social norms as guidance for his behavior. The Athenians ultimately used this against Socrates by charging him with the crime.

Socrates was sentenced to death by drinking poison.

The story of Socrates teaches us this—it is not socially acceptable to teach philosophy to children, unless they are your own children. Even if your intentions are pure, it is not socially acceptable, and you will likely face negative consequences.

Plato
Real name: Aristocles, "the best glory"
(aristos "best"   + kleos "glory, fame")
Nickname: Platon, "broad, broad shouldered"

Plato was a mystic. The nickname of "broad" is perfectly fitting for Plato, considering the breadth of topics that he discussed. Plato is regarded as the father of Western political science, but he also covered things like ethics, epistemology (study of knowledge), poetry, love, and the origin of our material reality.

Perhaps what Plato is most famous for is his ideas concerning metaphysics. The idea of immortality of the soul is foundational to all of his works. According to Plato, the pursuit of knowledge on earth is simply the process of remembering the knowledge that you possessed in heaven, before you came into embodiment.

It's worth mentioning that Plato had a more advanced set of teachings that he never wrote down. Plato preferred to share his most intimate knowledge with his students orally to avoid misunderstandings.

Plato was a very rational man, but what distinguishes him from Aristotle is his extensive use of the imagination. Whereas all of Aristotle's teachings were based on systematic, logical analysis of the material world, Plato's teachings were based much more on pure intuition. Aristotle's teachings are more practical for daily life, but Plato's teachings push you towards understanding life's greater mysteries.

Plato really challenged his students to stretch the limits of their minds beyond the physical world, in order to gain a stronger understanding of the physical world. Plato taught that understanding the non-material reality leads to a mastery over the material reality.

Theory of Forms
One of Plato's most popular ideologies was the theory of

Forms. In this system, we consider that the primary reality is NOT the material reality that we perceive with our senses. The material reality merely serves as a reflection of the primary reality.

The primary reality is the non-material reality that is only accessible through consciousness. This non-physical reality filters down to the physical plane of existence so that we can all perceive it with our physical senses.

Within the non-physical reality exists perfect abstract concepts—or Forms—that serve as the blueprint for our reality. The highest possible Forms are referred to as "Good". The Forms of the Good are perfect ideas for how life on earth should be, without suffering.

There exists lower Forms, such as greed or vanity, but the emphasis is on the higher forms because Plato wants to communicate that perfection on the material plane is possible. For Plato, the fact that humans can imagine a lifestyle free of suffering is proof that such a lifestyle exists, even if no one has personally experienced it in the real world.

Plato teaches that our material reality is basically a copy of a divine blueprint for a material reality. The divine blueprint is immaculate, but our material reality falls short of such perfection.

The difference between the perfect blueprint and our warped material reality is the imperfections that exist within the consciousness of humans, both on an individual and collective level, because as humans we create our material reality through our choices. That is, all material manifestations that are imperfect are consequences of imperfect human consciousness.

To illustrate the theory of Forms, we can apply the model to the concept of a friendship.

When analyzing any given friendship using Plato's theory of Forms, we seek to understand the non-material aspects of said friendship so that we can predict what will happen over time. In other words, we seek to understand the energetic relationship between the two friends. We could ask ourselves these questions:

How do their desires align with each other, both in the short term

and long term?
Do they share the same values and beliefs? What do they see as the purpose of life?

Once we have answered these questions, we can predict how the friendship will be outpictured in physicality over time. Based on the harmony (or conflict) between the energies of the two friends, we can predict whether or not the friendship will be a fruitful one.

This is merely one application of the theory of Forms. The theory can be applied in all aspects of life, in many creative ways.

Aristotle
Name: Aristoteles "the best aim"
(aristos "best" + telos "purpose, goal, end")

Aristotle is widely-considered the most influential philosopher from Ancient Greece, and maybe even the most influential non-religious thinker in the history of the world overall.

Aristotle wrote about an incredibly broad set of topics. This includes things such as physics, metaphysics, astronomy, biology, poetry, political science, and economics,

One of Aristotle's most prominent specialties was logic. He is known for popularizing the syllogism, which is a structured form of deductive reasoning where you draw a conclusion from a set of premises. This type of logic is commonly referred to as Aristotelean logic.

In order to gain a better understanding of the world, you break things down into smaller parts. You make observations about the world and use them to develop insights. Essentially, you accumulate more knowledge by systematically observing nature using Aristotelean logic.

Virtue Ethics
In his theory of virtue ethics, Aristotle describes a set of virtues as characteristics that all men should strive to embody if they

want to manifest a life of happiness.

Rather than presenting these virtues as simple concepts, he describes them as being the "golden mean" between two vices. Here's a few examples.

Deficiency	Virtue	Excess
Humility	Self-confidence	Arrogance
Cowardice	Courage	Rashness
Shamelessness	Modesty	Shyness

This model teaches us that it is only possible to embody the virtues by being aware of the balance that defines them. Mastery of all the virtues is achievable, but only through diligent effort. A lukewarm approach to ethics is likely to result in the embodiment of vices.

Aristotle encourages us to consistently live a contemplative life so that we can manifest positive experiences. By engaging in critical thinking, we can embody virtues and reap the rewards.

04 DEMOCRACY

Ancient Greece is widely considered the birthplace for Western political science because they were the first civilization to embrace *democracy*.

In other words, they were the first civilization to give the citizens the freedom to change society, a power which was previously only accessible to the power elite. This collective control has been an integral characteristic of Western civilization ever since.

Political Science

Before discussing Western political science, I want to make a clear distinction between *politics* and *political science*.

- Politics, from Greek *politika* ("affairs of the city"), from Greek *polis* ("city")
- Political science, from Greek *politika episteme* ("knowledge, science pertaining to the affairs of the city)

Political science is theoretical in nature. It is knowledge about how people interact collectively on a large scale and the different forms of government that can be used to cultivate civility. On the other hand, politics is the real world application of political science. Politics is an activity whereas political science is a system of thought.

Within political science, you might discuss how human choices could potentially derail a given system of government, but ultimately you don't know what kind of choices people will make. The behavior of individuals is not of primary relevance when studying political science. You are trying to gain a big-picture understanding of government with political science.

On the contrary, leaders in politics interact with the general population on a continual basis. Political power is based upon having the support of many people and therefore political leaders are forced adapt their policies according to collective desires.

Aristotle's Politics

Below you have three sets of government organized by centralization of power, with two forms of expression for each (positive and negative).

Ruled By	Positive Form	Negative Form
One	Monarchy	Tyranny
Few	Aristocracy	Oligarchy
Many	Polity (Civil State)	Democracy

This chart from Aristotle illustrates the idea that it is possible to have positive, virtuous systems of government, regardless of the centralization of power. However, the centralization of power become relevant when you have selfish behavior from the leaders.

In centralized government, corrupt leadership is difficult for the general population to stop due to lack of power. In decentralized government, the leaders are held accountable for their behavior by the general population.

The working class is vulnerable to unfair treatment in centralized governments, but they are much more protected in decentralized governments.

A polity—sometimes referred to as a constitutional democracy—is basically a civil organization within a community in which there is a clear structure to the government. One of the most important characteristics of a polity is the protection of minority groups from oppression. Aristotle describes democracy as a perversion of polity because of this potential oppression. Basically, all of the weaknesses for democracy involve minority groups being treated unfairly.

Growth

While a centralized power structure has certain perks, it limits the potential growth for most members of the group. When individuals have the opportunity to learn through their own creative choices they can make more rapid spiritual progress.

Within centralized power structures, most people don't have the opportunity to freely exercise their creativity because they are required to play a very rigid role within their society (usually labor-based). They don't even have a chance to make creative choices, and consequently their spiritual growth is slowed.

In decentralized power structures, you have a more diverse input of ideas. Not only does this improve the quality of the decision-making process within the power structures, but it also leads to accelerated spiritual growth for all of the members too.

I am not saying that monarchic or aristocratic societies are like prisons (although they certainly can be). I am merely saying that democratic power structures provide an environment for people to grow more rapidly, and this is why building one has been such a priority for Western nations.

Power Elite

First of all—on a *perfect* planet, no government is necessary because the people have a more sophisticated understanding of the laws of nature. Through perfect cooperation, the people generate an abundance of resources with no conflict. Any negative, self-serving behavior is automatically counteracted by natural forces.

On a more practical level, a democracy is the most ideal form of government for a planet like ours (specifically a constitutional democracy). This is for a number of reasons, but most importantly there exists no potential for the formation of the power elite in a democracy because all of the citizens are playing an active part in the decision making process.

Emotion vs. Logic

In general, popular votes through a direct democracy are at risk for producing decisions which are emotionally pacifying, rather than the most logical. Normally emotions are a good thing.

However, when it comes to making important governmental decisions, emotions can cloud the judgement of the majority.

This dynamic is commonly referred to as "mob think" or "mob rule". It refers to a potentially negative aspect of direct democracies where rational arguments are totally ineffective in swaying the popular opinion.

An individual can oftentimes become a **scapegoat** in a democracy if a collective mob decides the individual is to blame for whatever collective negative manifestations have come to surface in the public sphere. Even if the accusation isn't really justified, the scapegoat has no real chance to defend themselves because the majority of democratic voters have already made up their minds.

Public Education

Quite frankly, there is no guarantee that all of your citizens are well-educated.

In fact, this planet has a long history of being largely uneducated. Of course, you can define education in various ways, but I'm mainly referring to the population's ability to think rationally and solve their own problems. Comprehension of basic logic is something we take for granted in today's society, as it has been a skill unavailable to most people for most of history.

It's tough to say that a democracy is a great fit for societies where the majority of the population have not gained a basic mastery of logic. Problem solving requires critical thinking and if most people can't think critically then they aren't really helping to solve any problems. In this case it would actually be better to have decisions made by a small group of people who are most prepared to make objective governmental decisions for the betterment of the whole.

Now in the context of modern Western society, education has skyrocketed over the past century. And therefore you can argue that this specific weakness of a democracy is no longer relevant. However, from a historical perspective, public education has generally been lackluster and that's a major roadblock to manifesting a healthy democracy.

Leadership

In a direct democracy, all of the government's major decisions are determined by a popular vote. Every voter counts as equal, and therefore the only way to make changes are by winning a popular vote.

While this is usually a good thing, it can be problematic in the context of governmental decisions if the population is uneducated. If many of the democratic voters do not possess polished critical thinking skills, then they will voting based on emotions alone. And again, emotions are not a bad thing. However, as an individual leader, it is next to impossible to sway the populous if the people aren't willing to think critically about your proposals.

If you're someone who has genuinely innovative ideas in a democratic society, it can be very difficult to win over a majority of the voting population. Instead, ideas that are less eloquent, but more appealing to the mass consciousness, are likely to gain support.

05 REPUBLIC

Democracy vs. Republic

The word "democracy" comes from Greek roots meaning "the people have power, the people rule" and it describes how the ancient Greeks structured their governments. The people voted *directly* on decisions being made in their city-state.

The Romans popularized a different—but in many ways similar—form of government known as the **republic**. The word "republic" comes from Latin roots meaning "public entity, public interest" (note the word *public* in re*public*). A republic is a system of government that uses elected representatives to vote on decisions, with the consent of the public.

A proper republic is similar to a democracy because the government is structured specifically to give power to the *entire* population, as opposed to a small number of people.

The key difference between the two is that the general population doesn't vote for matters of policy directly in a republic like they do in a pure democracy. However—in theory—the decisions being made by republican leaders should always align with the best interests of the entire population. Therefore, the general population does have collective control over the government indirectly in a republic. Republics are commonly referred to as indirect democracies.

Public Entity

The transition from more centralized governments to a republic has been a monumental turning point for many nations in history because traditionally everything in the nation—land, infrastructure, resources, and to some degree even the people themselves—was the property of the ruling class.

This transition is roughly comparable to a private corporation transitioning to a public corporation. With a public corporation, all business decisions need to be made with the shareholders' best interest in mind. Likewise, with a republic, all government decisions need to be made with the public's best interest in mind.

Although a republic isn't a full-blown democracy where the people operate the government directly, it is still a major progression from more centralized traditional power structures. Most importantly, the general population in a republic doesn't feel like the property of the power elite.

In a true republic, the people are supposed to be free. The common man may still be required to work, but the leaders in a republic don't have unquestionable authority like they do in a monarchy or oligarchy.

Aristocracy

Many republics do use democratic processes to elect their representatives, including the USA. However, that doesn't necessarily need to be the case.

- In a *democratic republic*, the general population casts votes to choose the representatives.
- In an *aristocratic republic*, a group of elders vote to choose which children should be given educational privileges based on the quality of their consciousness as a youth. These children then grow up and qualify to become representatives through merit.
- In an *oligarchic republic*, a privileged ruling class selects the representatives.

In general, republics exist on a spectrum ranging from democratic to oligarchic.

On a surface level, republican leaders can be elected democratically through popular votes or they can be appointed by powerful individuals Aristocratic representatives are chosen based on merit and oligarchic representatives are chosen based on other factors.

Beneath the surface, republican representatives can cast votes based on the desires of the ruling class (oligarchic) or based on the desires of the entire population (democratic), or anywhere in between. A republic can easily be labelled as democratic on the surface, but function more like an oligarchy in reality if the republican leaders are loyal to a power elite.

While ideally there shouldn't be much discrepancy between the desires of the ruling class and the desires of the entire population, when it comes to distribution of resources, there can be plenty of disagreements!

An aristocratic republic is the ideal form of republic in which the republican leaders choose representatives based on a process of philosophical contemplation. This decision making process isn't one which can be clearly defined in terms of political science because it takes so many variables into account in each individual circumstance. Aristocratic republican leaders should actually transcend the desires of both the ruling class and the general population when seeking to make the highest possible choices. Aristocratic leaders operate a republic according to universal principles.

Plato's Republic

The ideology of a republic can be traced back to Plato and his work titled, *Republic*. This piece is a dialogue where Socrates discusses the ideal form of government with various other citizens.

The original Greek title of Plato's work is *Politeia* (Polity). The title *Res Publica* is a Latin title which was later applied to Plato's *Politeia* because it fit the Roman idea of a republic.

Ironically, Plato's republic can accurately be described as an *aristocracy*, although its title literally indicates that it's a *polity* (Aristotle's positive form of democracy). This illustrates that there really shouldn't be much difference between a proper aristocracy (rule by few) and a polity (rule by many).

In Plato's republic, individuals are placed into a three-tiered structure based on their attained level of consciousness. The three groups are the Golden Class (Leaders), the Silver Class (Administrators), and the Bronze Class (Laborers).

The people are placed into the appropriate class during their youth based on careful observation from the elders. The elders track the learning of individuals during their early years in order to gain an understanding of the spiritual maturity of each student, and then the elders make placements accordingly. Students receive systematic education throughout their formative years based on their designated class.

NOTE: It's difficult to appreciate Plato's Republic without understanding the metaphysical basis of his ideas. Plato believed in the immortality of the soul and reincarnation, which are both foundational ideas to his proposed government.

This is similar to the American educational system, where students earn access to higher education and scholarships based on individual merit. However, the idea of merit in Plato's republic is more *qualitative*, as opposed to the *quantitative* standards used in modern public education (GPA and test scores).

In practical terms, schools in Plato's republic would be more interested in a student's essays than his or her test scores. In other words, school wouldn't be quite as competitive as it is today.

Gold

Referred to as philosopher kings by Plato, the Golden Class is given the lengthiest and most complex education so that they may eventually become wise decision-makers for the entire republic.

This is by far the smallest class proportionally to the entire population. The Golden Class is similar to royalty, however they are placed into their privileged position based on aristocratic measures, not based on bloodlines as with a monarchy.

The Golden Class consists of natural problem solvers who possess creative thinking skills which can't be fully taught by an external teacher. Even from a young age, golden children have a natural ability to think outside of the box. Although the philosopher kings are the most privileged, they are actually the hardest-working group as they are always contemplating and self-transcending their present state of consciousness.

The concept of a philosopher king is a subtle, but powerful description of the ideal republican leader. In short, republican leaders will always act in the best interest of the public because it's the *wisest* thing to do. That is, they don't choose their behaviors as leaders based on a sense of obligation to the public, but rather they choose to behave in the best interest of the public because it is in harmony with their own individual enlightened self-interest.

In addition, if the Golden Class fails to act in the best interest of the people, then technically the government no longer functions as a proper republic. You would have an oligarchic regime cloaked as a republic, because the essence of republican leadership is to serve the publc.

Silver

The Silver Class receives a sizable education, particularly in logic and ethics, so that they may properly administer the choices made by the Golden Class. The Silver Class also works to acquire the ability to fairly mediate disputes among the Bronze Class.

Generally, people who possess advanced labor skills belong in the Silver Class because they can be effective leaders for economic production. They are vital members of society who have the responsibility to sustainably organize production and continuously energize the labor workers. The warriors are also members of the Silver Class.

The Silver Class is known for the sense of *passion* that fuels their behavior. Individuals who are particularly ambitious or have a strong desire to manifest excellence are ideal leaders for the Silver Class. These people are loyal, fervent followers of the philosopher kings who are willing to fearlessly protect the republic, whether it be from internal uprisings or external military attacks.

Some people are better suited for the Silver Class than the Golden Class, even if they are exceptionally intelligent. That is, an individual may exhibit a strong willpower to learn, but the modes of thinking available to the Golden Class are difficult to learn in short periods of time, i.e. a single lifetime. Individuals in the Silver Class may possess a strong intellect, but individuals in the Golden Class possess a strong intellect *and* an extraordinary level of innate wisdom.

Bronze

The Bronze Class is the majority of the population and they are mostly responsible for the daily labor. Over time, society has developed complex economies with specialization of labor, but traditionally the Bronze Class is responsible for agricultural production. It's the original labor!

Whereas the Golden Class acts based on *wisdom* and the Silver Class acts based on *passion*, the Bronze Class acts according to their *appetite* (food, drink, reproduction, money, etc.). The Bronze Class is generally uneducated and therefore they don't possess refined thinking skills.

This does NOT mean that the Bronze Class is unintelligent. All members of the Bronze Class possess a fully-functioning intuition and basic critical thinking skills. However, they simply do not receive as lengthy of an education as the Golden and Silver Classes.

Individuals are considered members of the Bronze Class by default if they are primarily motivated by making money, as opposed to a higher purpose.

Free Time

The most important distinction to be made among the three classes is the amount of free time allotted to each class.

The Golden Class is considered the most privileged because they are allowed to spend most of their time learning and contemplating, instead of laboring. The Silver Class is generally busy administrating daily affairs in the community, but they aren't typically performing manual labor. Meanwhile, the entire republic is dependent on the labor of the Bronze Class to produce successful harvests!

I want to make it very clear that in a republic, there is not supposed to a sense of superiority from members the higher classes towards members of the lower classes. Specifically, the Bronze citizens are not to be viewed as less valuable members of society than Golden and Silver citizens.

Rather, the leaders are simply more advanced spiritually. Therefore, the Golden Class is given the privilege of free time so that they can focus on inner levels and consequently use their wisdom to lead the republic. The leaders should hold a servant leadership attitude towards their privileged status and be chiefly concerned with raising the overall spiritual awareness of the common people.

Bronze and Silver citizens are simply at an earlier stage of the spiritual path where they are still learning about the universal principles that govern earthly life. They are still refining their psyches.

Strengths of a Republic

- ☐ Public ownership of government prevents tyranny or pure oligarchy
- ☐ Combination of centralized and decentralized decision making
- ☐ To some extent, requires rational justification of choices from leaders (not required in monarchy or oligarchy)
- ☐ Privileges allow leaders to devote their lives to continuous learning, as opposed to physical labor
- ☐ Governmental decisions are debated among groups of individuals who have high levels of philosophical understanding and broad vision
- ☐ Clear division of labor produces reliable agricultural yields for entire population
- ☐ Allows for military personnel to spend a significant amount of time training for battle
- ☐ Stratification of society incentivizes individuals to pursue learning in order to become leaders

Weaknesses of a Republic

- ☐ Potential for an elitist mindset, or a sense of inherent superiority, to develop among the ruling class
- ☐ Leaders may prioritize securing election in contrast to serving the *entire* population, (i.e. being overly-influenced by wealthy groups or acting without concern for minority groups)
- ☐ Stratified social structure can make social mobility difficult if leaders abandon the attitude of servant leadership
- ☐ Bronze Class is oftentimes overworked and unfairly compensated for their labor
- ☐ Framework assumes a significant gap in spiritual maturity between leaders and general population, which is becomingly increasingly non-existent in modern civilization.

06 MIDDLE AGES

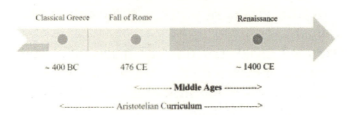

As mentioned in Chapter 3, the timespan between ancient Greece and the Renaissance was somewhat of an ideological vacuum in the Western world. Throughout that entire period, practically all of secular education was based on the teachings of Aristotle. Students were trained to utilize Aristotle's methods of logic and in turn contribute knowledge to humanity by systematically studying the world around them.

The period from Greece to the Renaissance is ~1800 years. In comparison, all of Western history (Greece to present day) is ~2400 years. Aristotelian curriculum was the basis of mainstream secular education for roughly 75% of Western history.

As you can see in the timeline above, the Middle Ages is said to stretch roughly a millennium from the fall of the Roman Empire to the Italian Renaissance. Another way to frame this is that the Middle Ages are the bridge between the classical world and the modern world.

Catholic Church

The word *catholic* comes from the Greek root *katholikos* meaning "universal".

A universal church could never become geographically centralized in one location.
A catholic church is a gathering of people who acknowledge universal principles, and not a physical establishment.

East-West Schism

Christianity began as a decentralized spiritual movement comprised of various Jewish-Christian sects.

About three centuries after the ministry of Jesus, orthodox Christianity was unified into a single group when the Roman emperor held an assembly for Catholic bishops to meet and come to an agreement on official church doctrines. Later that century, a different Roman emperor decreed that Christianity was the official state religion of the Roman Empire.

More assemblies were held in Rome over the next few centuries to resolve various theological disputes, but around the year 1000 a permanent fracture was formed within the Catholic Church.

The Eastern Orthodox Church split from the Roman Catholic Church at this time for a number of reasons, including both political and theological disagreements. The Eastern Orthodox Church is also known as the Greek Orthodox Church because they favor studying Greek scriptures, as opposed to the Latin translations used by the Roman Catholic Church.

The issue of papal primacy was particularly relevant to the schism as respect for the pope's spiritual authority disintegrated within the Eastern Orthodox community. However, the most significant disagreement was based around the nature of the Holy Trinity.

The Roman Catholics promoted Trinity where the Father and the Son are considered equals. The Holy Spirit is considered to emanate from both the Father and the Son, according to Roman Catholic doctrine.

The Orthodox Church favored a trinity which placed supreme emphasis on the Father. In other words, the Orthodox Church believed that the Father existed at a point in time independently of the Son and the Holy Spirit, and therefore the Father should be elevated relative to the other two.

Another way to word this is that Roman Catholic doctrine emphasizes the unity of the Holy Trinity, whereas the Orthodox doctrine emphasizes the distinctions that exist within the Trinity.

Catholic Europe

The power structure of the Roman Catholic Church is unique to world history. In effect, this church was set up as a super-monarchy, so to speak, uniting all of Europe.

With a normal monarchy, the kingdom is governed by the earthly authority of the royal family, typically with the assumption that the royal family is divinely favored.

With the Roman Catholic Church, Europe was governed by the spiritual authority of the church, based on the idea that Jesus intended for a pope to be the chief representative of Christ on earth.

As Christians believe Jesus to the key to their salvation, that designation was conferred unto the pope in Roman Catholicism. Therefore, the majority of Europeans eventually came to see the pope and the Roman Catholic Church as having the authority to grant salvation.

This power dynamic, where the people believed they must serve an earthly authority in order to achieve eternal salvation, is not good.

The unity provided by Roman Catholicism did have positive effects on European life. However, the harsh reality is that the centralized power structure within the church led to abuses of power by Catholic leaders. The abuses of power within the Roman Catholic Church continued to snowball for centuries without much opposition and inevitably eroded the quality of life for Europeans.

Dark Ages

The Middle Ages have popularly been referred to as the "Dark Ages".

An academic explanation of the Dark Ages describes it as being "dark" because there aren't many primary documents found from this time period. In other words, it is called "dark" because we don't have much physical evidence on which to base our understanding.

The title of Dark Ages also describes the philosophical decline of Europe during Middle Ages. More specifically, Europe exhibited a decline in enlightenment because the people built centralized power structures during the Middle Ages.

This was in opposition to the positive trend in the classical world where democratic principles, decentralized power structures, and the spirit of individualism were prevalent.

So, although the Middle Ages were really a period of considerable peace and abundance, the centralization of power structures during this period were counterproductive to the spiritual growth of the European people. Instead of continuing to integrate more democratic principles into society after the Roman Empire, Europe became controlled by monarchies on a local level and by a centralized spiritual authority on a collective level.

Feudalism

This centralization of power is very clearly displayed by the economic system of feudalism, which was very popular during the Middle Ages. Here's a simple representation of the power structure that existed within European feudal society:

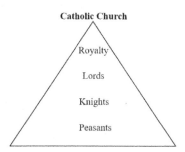

And since the Catholic Church was viewed as the earthly representative of Christ, European kings were subservient to the church. In reality, there were many power struggles between the pope and kings, but in general the kings respected the authority of the pope.

On a local level, all land was owned by the royal family in a feudal society. Plots of land were divided among lords who were favored by the monarchy. It was expected that the lords would administrate agricultural production on the land and pay taxes to the monarchy. The knights were professionally trained soldiers who served in the royal military.

Although there was a multi-tiered power structure, it's important to understand that only small fraction of the population were lords and knights. The overwhelming majority of European citizens were peasants/serfs who were tasked with farming the land in exchange for food, shelter, and military protection.

The worst part about feudalism is that the leaders had little to no respect for the labor of the farmers. Most farmers weren't technically slaves, but they didn't have many ways to secure their livelihood other than by working the land. And although the farmers were the ones who were physically growing the food they were only allowed to keep a sliver of the harvest for themselves and their families. Most of the harvest was collected as taxes by the power elite.

So here you had an economic system where the majority of society was constantly laboring, but they were consistently denied the rewards of their labors. In essence, the power elite treated the working class as farm animals whose only purpose in life was to produce agricultural yields. The leaders had no respect for the spiritual growth of the farmers.

Needless to say this sort of society is totally out of alignment with divine will, but again, the centralized power structure of feudalism made it incredibly difficult for the common man to demand change.

Black Death

Although there wasn't as much spiritual growth in the Middle Ages compared to the classical period or the Renaissance, it's inaccurate to say life was totally miserable in the Middle Ages.

People in Europe enjoyed simple lives based around farming and their Christian faith. This status quo persisted for centuries, until abuses of power became too much of a burden on the lower class. Towards the end of the Middle Ages, the peasants were suffering tremendously. The European power elite was perfectly content at this point, but the peasants were being pushed to their limits.

Things continued to get worse in Europe and the people eventually experienced severe famine and disease, culminating in the Black Death. The Black Death was a period of disease in Europe where roughly half of the entire population died.

Some people believe that the Black Death manifested a consequence of the spiritual conditions of Europe. That is, widespread disease was a message from the universe that the European people needed to re-examine their fundamental approach to life.

It's safe to say that everything was not okay at the end of the Middle Ages in Europe!

07 RENAISSANCE

During Middle Ages, Europe gradually became the most powerful region of the world.

The influence of the Roman Empire and the Catholic Church spread across all of Europe and many new cities were built in the process. Rome had exceptionally advanced infrastructure for that time period. The Roman civilization was full of well-built roads and aqueducts which allowed increased urbanization.

As sophisticated technology expanded geographically across Europe, naturally there was an increased production of resources. In particular, better agricultural technology gave rise to more abundant harvests.

Although the production of resources was accelerating rapidly, the European power structure remained completely centralized around the Roman Empire and the Roman Catholic Church.

Taxes

As you might imagine, the economic control of the Roman Empire over Europe continuously became more intense.

Not only did the Roman Church continue to raise taxes, but the local kings also had a tendency to raise taxes on the peasants too. The tax collections were portions of agricultural production that were taken from the peasants during each harvest and collected by military officers.

The problem with taxing the farmers so heavily is that sometimes there wouldn't be enough food left over for the farmers to feed their own families. The taxes took priority over feeding the peasants.

There were more reasons for frustration in Europe, such as religious intolerance from the ruling class, but the economic inequality was completely unsustainable. The working class was not being given a reasonable share of their agricultural production.

More Books

The major advancement in technology that really lit the fuse for the Renaissance was the printing press. It's difficult to overstate the impact that this machine had on the European power structure over the next few centuries.
I'll list just a few of the reasons why the printing press was pivotal.

1) <u>Increase in literacy</u>

Books were much rarer before the printing press and typically only the upper class had access to libraries. The majority of the population didn't even come in contact with books on a regular basis. With the mass production of books, the average citizen had a much greater incentive to learn how to read.

2) <u>Raise in vibration</u>

Before the printing press, the only ideas that passed through people's minds were ideas that they encountered on a physical basis or through word of mouth.

With an increased number of books, the average person could potentially expose themselves to a much wider range of ideas over a relatively short period of time.

3) <u>Reading of scriptures</u>

Prior to the Renaissance, only the most educated members of society could read holy books because they were typically written in Greek or Latin.

Once the Bible was translated into many different languages and mass-produced with the printing press, there was a significantly higher number of people reading the scriptures independently.

4) <u>Decentralization of sharing information</u>

Mass production of printed materials, and thus the potential to spread information publicly, dramatically altered the political landscape of Europe. With the printing press, minority groups gained new ways to communicate and share information without the need to meet in physical assemblies. This is particularly important considering there was so much religious oppression in Europe at this point in time.

Inquisition

When you combine the growing economic inequality in Europe with an increasingly educated population, naturally the common people started to question authority figures.

There was a tug-of-war, so to speak, in Europe between the ruling class and the common people. The more the commoners rebelled against the orthodox belief systems and challenged the leaders, the more likely the ruling class was to persecute them.

The Roman Catholic Church had been the centerpiece of European culture for over a millennia, but repeated abuses of power by Catholic leaders gradually eroded the trust of the European people.

As a result, many Europeans were attracted to the classical humanities. Again, the humanities were created as a path to knowledge independent of divinity.

Other individuals didn't respond to this situation by abandoning religion, but rather by challenging spiritual integrity of the Catholic Church. In other words, they believed the Catholic Church didn't embody the true spirit of Christianity.

Either way, a very large portion of European citizens had grown unsatisfied with the Catholic Church and were seeking ways to grow independently from it.

Italian Renaissance

Italian Renaissance is typically described as the initial stage of the European Renaissance and it is characterized by a preference for classical approaches to learning in contrast with religious approaches.

To some extent, the humanities had been buried by Catholic doctrines during the Middle Ages. During the Italian Renaissance, a large number of individuals returned the humanitarian philosophies that were once so treasured in Greece and Rome.

The word *renaissance* is French for "rebirth" and it it describes the revival of enlightenement that occurred in Europe.

Florence

The Medici were an extremely influential family from Florence who are often credited for sparking the Italian Renaissance altogether. Florence was the cultural hub of the Italian Renaissance and the Medici were the political rulers of Florence for centuries.

Most of the famous Renaissance artists—Leonardo, Michelangelo, Raphael, Donatello, etc.—were able to spend all of their time on artwork thanks to the patronage of the Medici family.

The Medici family had a particularly strong attraction to the metaphysical philosophy of Plato. Interestingly, the Latin word *medici* means "physician".

While we typically attribute to the Renaissance a renewal of classical ideas in such as architecture, literature, painting, sculpture—the most critical element of the Renaissance was a refreshed perspective on healthcare.

The medical methods that were used in the classical world and renewed in Renaissance Europe are not very similar to modern Western medicine which is based on scientific materialism. In fact, classical medicine is more closely aligned with Eastern medical traditions, which place a greater emphasis on the psyche as opposed to the physical symptoms.

Divine Comedy

The *Divine Comedy* is an epic poem written by Dante Alighieri and split into three books. In the poem, Dante himself travels through the three regions of our universe: hell (inferno), purgatory, and heaven (paradise).

The poem is a comedy because it fits the classical definition of comedy—namely that it has a happy ending and Dante ends up in heaven.

Most of the images of heaven in hell that you see in pop culture (movies, cartoons, etc.) actually owe their origin to Dante's *Divine Comedy*. That's not to say that heaven and hell are not biblical, but rather that many images associated with them come from this poem.

For example, the idea of standing in a fiery inferno next to the devil as a depiction of hell comes from *Divine Comedy*.

In addition, Dante's work was revolutionary because it was one of the first major pieces of artwork to criticize the Catholic Church. In the poem, Catholic priests are depicted as suffering in hell alongside other sinners. The priests are punished for their abuses of power and are punished accordingly in hell.

Northern Renaissance

While the Italian Renaissance was related to the revival of the classics, the northern European citizens took a slightly difference approach towards learning. The classics were also influential in Northern Europe, but the major trend that characterizes the Northern Renaissance is a re-examination of the foundations of Christianity.

Northern Europeans—particularly in England, France, and Germany —placed a higher value on religious texts than classical texts. The classical texts were helpful because they helped understand the context of early Christian doctrines, but overall the culture in Northern Europe became *more* religious during Renaissance than it was during the Middle Ages.

Whereas Italian Renaissance thinkers studied humanism to move away from religion, the Northern Renaissance thinkers combined humanism with religion to form their own understanding of Christianity, independently from the Catholic Church.

In other words, Christian mysticism rapidly grew in popularity during the Northern Renaissance.

Protestant Reformation

Eventually, there came a development known as the Protestant Reformation in which a critical mass of Europeans formally challenged the authority of the Catholic Church to define Christian life. This church practically had maintained a monopoly over Christian life for over a millennia, but the unified organization was disbanded during the Reformation.

The Reformation was a direct consequence of increased literacy in Europe. It was only possible for independent voices to gain such widespread support from European through indirect means. Centralized power structures had traditionally prevented anti-Catholic "heretics" from influencing the public.

Protestant leaders published pamphlets to share their objections of the Catholic Church with all of Europe. This is clearly demonstrated in the life of Martin Luther, who is usually credited with jump-starting the Reformation by publishing a key critique of the Catholic Church.

Universe Cities

Renaissance culture included the growth of public, secular institutions of higher learning. The university—or universe city—has roots that go back to Ancient Greece, but universities were not widely popular until the Renaissance.

Renaissance universities are where individuals went to receive an education based around individualism, as opposed to religious collectivism. This individualistic curriculum in Renaissance universities was largely equivalent to the classical curriculum.

The purpose of a university is to produce enlightened students. In other words, universities are designed to fill students with the knowledge that, through proper effort, they can genuinely improve their own quality of life.

Early Modern Literature

One of the benefits of the printing press was not only the increase in the volume of books, but also the potential that it gave the average person to write books.

Prior to the Renaissance, the only stories that circulated within the collective consciousness were stories that had been passed down throughout generations. In other words, a story could only survive if it was extremely popular enough among the people that it was either written down or simply passed on through oral tradition.

Other times, literature could survive if it had a significant degree of practical value (religious and philosophical texts).

With the Renaissance, a new genre of literature rapidly gained popularity—novels. In short, early modern writers were much more motivated to create unique stories out of thin air because of the explosion of the book market. Novels have had an immeasurable influence on the growth of the collective imagination over the past few centuries.

Over time, the themes explored in early modern literature became more feminist, relative to most traditional epics which focused on heroic acts of warriors. New themes challenged traditional patriarchal worldviews and questioned the woman's subordinate role in society. In addition, literature from this period also began to explore the feminine aspect of the man, i.e. the spiritual part of the self that exists in all people: man and woman.

Shakespeare

Another common form of literature from the early modern period was the play. Easily the most influential playwright in the English language was William Shakespeare, who truly embodied the enlightened spirit of the English Renaissance.

The historical biography and personal identity of William Shakespeare remains largely a mystery. However, legend has it that the word "Shakespeare" is a reference to the brandishing of a spear by the Greek goddess Pallas Athena. A goddess of weaving and warfare among other things, Athena was known to shake her spear at fools who disrespected the gods.

Shakespeare had an incredibly broad mind, and a clear understanding of metaphysics. Shakespeare was able to create and intertwine characters which were completely lifelike. Shakespeare's work addresses universal themes that strike specific chords in the audience's psyche, regardless of what culture the audience hails from.

Shakespeare was the first great psychologist!

08 SCIENTIFIC REVOLUTION

1. <u>Renaissance</u> - Describes the revival of humanism after the Middle Ages. Secular study of human affairs was a shift from a Christian study of human affairs. Overall, Europe became more educated.
2. <u>Scientific Revolution</u> - Movement which proposed that knowledge could be increased through human reason alone, independently of religious or classical sources. Initially associated with inductive reasoning, the Scientific Revolution eventually trended towards empiricism and the scientific method.
3. <u>Enlightenment</u> - Much broader in scope than the Scientific Revolution. Enlightenment thinkers applied inductive reasoning to all areas of human life.

    The Scientific Revolution is an integral component of Western history. The philosophies produced this from this period were pivotal to the progression of Western education as a whole.

    The most important thing to grasp is the difference between *deductive reasoning* and *inductive reasoning*, and how they both relate to human life.

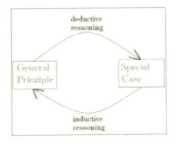

Deductive vs Inductive

    Deductive reasoning describes humans using logic to move from universal principles to particular instances. In other words, using common wisdom to make choices in life.

By definition, the premises in deductive reasoning should guarantee the truth of the conclusion.

Inductive reasoning describes humans using logic to move from particular instances to universal principles. In other words, using your experiences (or data) to make choices in life.

By definition, the premises in inductive reasoning do NOT guarantee the truth of the conclusion, but only support it.

Aristotle and Organon

Aristotle is created the formal systems of logic that were used for most of Western history. His collection of logic is titled *Organon,* which is a Greek word meaning "tool or instrument". This word is significant because it reflects a sense of modesty in Aristotle's logical method, framing it as only one of presumably numerous tools to be used by philosophers.

In particular, Aristotle's method of syllogism was the dominant tool used by academics all the way from ancient Greece until the Scientific Revolution.

The word syllogism comes from the Greek root *sullogismos* which means "inference, conclusion". *Sullogismos* is the word used by Aristotle to describe his deductive method, as the words deductive and inductive did not exist in the Greek language.

While to modern people Aristotle's deductive method might not seem important, it should be noted that there were no formal systems of logic beforehand.

There were philosophers who discussed logic prior to Aristotle, but there was no widely-accepted system of logic until Aristotle. In other words, there was no way to coordinate formal debates without bias until Aristotle produced his *Organon*.

Aristotle briefly mentions inductive reasoning in his *Organon,* but not nearly to the same extent as deductive reasoning. Nonetheless, inductive reasoning plays an integral in Aristotelean logic, a fact which has oftentimes been overlooked by scholars.

Aristotle uses the Greek word *"epagoge"* to describe inductive reasoning, and this word means "to bring in, to bring to a conclusion".

For Aristotle, inductive reasoning was particularly useful in two ways.

>1) To make rational decisions in moments of uncertainty with limited information, as long as deductive first principles are not violated.
>
>2) To verify the deductive first principles. Sufficient induction should prove the truth of the first principles.

Aristotle describes inductive reasoning as a supplement to deductive reasoning

Medieval Scholasticism

The words school and scholasticism both come from the same Greek root of *skhole*, which interestingly means "leisure or rest [from labor]".

During the Middle Age, most of the academics were actually Christian monks (from Greek *monachos* "solitary, alone") who lived in monasteries. The monasteries coordinated a labor distribution among the monks to ensure agricultural production. The monks used their remaining free time mostly for prayer and meditation.

Scholasticism was basically deductive reasoning applied to human life, with premises based on Christian theology. That is, medieval scholars combined Catholic beliefs with the deductive method provided by Aristotle.

Commentaries were a very common form of scholarship during this time period. For example, individuals would take information from Biblical or classical sources and apply it to their own life so that contemporary citizens could benefit from it. Other times, scholars produced commentaries that were critiques of popular doctrines.

Inductive reasoning was not a major part of scholastic culture during the Middle Ages.

Research Universities

As discussed last chapter, universities multiplied in quantity during the Renaissance. Initially, the curriculum of universities was based purely around philosophy. Again, this doesn't mean philosophy was the only discipline. Rather, all of the disciplines were subsumed by philosophy. All higher education was geared towards the pursuit of wisdom.

As the Scientific Revolution worked through Europe, universities became increasingly focused on scientific experimentation. More specifically, universities became dominated by the scientific method and empiricism. This is not necessarily a bad thing. However, as the Scientific Revolution progressed, many universities gradually moved away from nurturing enlightenment and instead became hyper-focused on scientific research.

This is a trend that has snowballed into modern universities. In modern terms, many universities currently place a primary emphasis on STEM (science, technology, engineering, and mathematics) learning, and a secondary emphasis philosophical learning. This is totally off-base from the original blueprint and purpose of universities.

Novum Organum

A British philosopher named Francis Bacon published a work entitled *Novum Organum*, which is translated into English as "New Method". *Novum Organum* is a philosophical treatise which primarily argues for the pursuit of knowledge using only inductive reasoning.

This was revolutionary idea because, historically speaking, philosophers considered using inductive reasoning as an independent path to knowledge as a fruitless exercise.

Bacon proposed that through a careful and extremely structured process of observing nature, humans could accumulate data over time. This data could then be used to gain insights, but only if it was collected using proper technique!

Bacon's ideas proved to be foundational to the subsequent scientific revolution and he is often characterized as having been opposed to Aristotle. Although Bacon did choose the title *Novum*

Organum as a clear allusion to Aristotle's *Organon,* it's slightly off-base to say that Bacon was opposed to Aristotle. Likewise, it's erroneous to say Aristotle was opposed to inductive reasoning.

We must remember the original meaning of the Greek word *Organon* ("tool, instrument") and the sense of modesty that it carries. Just as Aristotle proposed his *Organon* as a tool for philosophers to use, Francis Bacon proposed his *Novum Organum* as a tool to be paired with Aristotle's method. The two methods are complementary, and not conflicting.

Scientific Materialism

The Scientific Method is NOT the pinnacle of learning !!

The inductive method proposed by Bacon quickly gained popularity because it was a perfect fit for the refreshed individualistic mindset that was common in Europe at this time. The method was a way for people to develop new knowledge by themselves, without the help of an authority figure.

A philosophy known as empiricism, which is a form of inductive reasoning where all data is collected through *the physical senses*, eventually developed in Europe. Empiricism is the basic foundation of the "scientific method" that is taught in universities today.

A major problem with empiricism is that it eventually led to a popular worldview in Western culture known as scientific materialism.

Whereas empiricism merely describes using sensory data to gain knowledge, scientific materialism describes the belief that nothing exists beyond the material world. In other words, there does not exist any sort of spiritual reality beyond what humans can directly perceive, or measure with their physical senses.

Scientific materialism is a belief that became more prevalent in Europe during the Scientific Revolution and, along with religion, scientific materialism has become one of the two dominant worldviews in modern society.

Never before in history had there been a widespread belief

that nothing existed beyond the physical world. That is, spirituality had always been a part of human life until the development of scientific materialism.

Natural Philosophy

Before the Scientific Revolution—physics was philosophy, natural philosophy to be exact. The word physics comes from Greek *physikos* meaning "relating to nature".

Traditionally, natural philosophy was primarily focused with human life, and not with inanimate matter. That's not to say there weren't natural philosophers who studied ecology, geology, etc. However, when you read about Aristotle's physics, for example, you need to approach it with an open mind.

With natural philosophy from the past, you're not going to get much value from it if you are thinking in terms of modern physics. To some extent, natural philosophy from classical antiquity can be described as being tailored to the mythical consciousness which ruled the ancient world.

Subjects such as alchemy simply do not fit into the modern scientific materialist mindset.

Natural Science

When the modern scientific method gained popularity and you had names like Galileo and Newton publishing popular treatises on physics, the public perception of physics began to morph.

Physics was no longer was no longer primarily concerned with human life, but instead became primarily focused on studying inanimate matter. The public perception of physics became more empirical and less philosophical.

This trend carried throughout the remainder of Western history in the public sphere, where the scientific materialist mindset is still so prevalent today. In modern education, we have natural sciences which are based on the scientific method. The natural sciences essentially replaced natural philosophy in schools, although natural science is materialistic and natural philosophy is not materialistic.

09 ENLIGHTENMENT

Usually the Enlightenment is linked together with the Scientific Revolution because both of the movements promoted rational thinking and inductive reasoning. Although there is significant overlap, there are many key distinctions to be made.

- ☐ Classics and Middle Ages: **Deductive Reasoning**
- ☐ Scientific Revolution: **Narrow Inductive Reasoning**
- ☐ Enlightenment: **Broad Inductive Reasoning**

Diversity

The scientific method basically consists of conducting experiments with a strict structure and very careful observation. In addition, scientific experiments need to be generic enough so that they can be replicated—infinitely in theory—and produce the same results (a concept known as external validity).

This procedure is great for gaining a greater understanding of how the material world works at a fundamental level because matter always behaves the same way. Therefore, external validity isn't a problem in the context of physical science.

External validity is a key concept because when you start applying the scientific method to humans, it becomes a major obstacle. In other words, it's very difficult to collect data that applies to real life in a purely universal fashion when you are studying humans.

In short, humans are just too diverse. Not only on a physical level, but especially on a mental level. When you factor in multiple people (friendship, marriage, family, society), the diversity grows exponentially.

Freethinking

By definition, inductive reasoning describes the formation

of insights from the accumulation of data. As previously discussed, the scientific method is a narrow form of inductive reason where you are collecting a very specific type of data.

The term broad induction contrasts with the narrow scientific method which has become so popular. Broad induction is a term that describes the formation of insights from the accumulation of data in general, in contrast to the specific type of data that the scientific method requires. In other words, broad induction is a much more abstract process than the scientific method and with broad induction you are able to use a much, much broader potential set of data.

With the increase in books during the Renaissance, this broad form of inductive reasoning became relevant because the common individual had access to a large amount of new information. This same dynamic exists in modern society where the common individual has access to a virtually infinite set of information on the internet.

Globalization

Not only did Europe experience the return of classical Greek and Roman thought during the Renaissance, but European thought was also influenced by Eastern doctrines by the time of the Enlightenment. That is, Enlightenment thinkers became progressively more familiar with the more mystical systems of thought that have developed over the course of history in the Eastern hemisphere.

In short, Enlightenment thinkers began to synthesize global doctrines in ways that transcended the orthodox religious teachings in Europe. This is a very natural development, especially considering the new plethora of global information available to the public during this time period.

Liberty

On a *basic* level, the Enlightenment advocated the application of *human reason*. While Enlightenment thinkers were certainly proponents of the scientific method, there are much broader applications of human reason, too.

On a *political* level, the key dynamic of the Enlightenment was the shift from centralized government (monarchy, oligarchy) to decentralized government (democracy, republic). Although democratic principles did become more important during the Enlightenment, it's worth noting that almost all of the democratic thinkers during this time period were republican.

On a *philosophical* and most consequential level, the primary ideal of the Enlightenment was **LIBERTY**. Liberty specifically refers to the freedom to use your time however you like, without interference from the government. "Do as you wish, and harm none."

~~~~~~

It can be very useful to think of the Enlightenment as a general concept so that you can compare it to other chunks of time in world history.

However, I want to go into a bit of detail describing the national variations of the Enlightenment that existed in Europe. The beautiful thing about the Enlightenment was that there was an incredibly diverse set of unique cultures that were all growing simultaneously.

Whereas you had a relatively centralized European culture with Catholicism in the Middle Ages, European culture became much more varied during the Enlightenment.

~~~~~~

Dutch Enlightenment

The Netherlands didn't actually experience the Enlightenment in the same way as the rest of Europe. Rather, shortly after the Renaissance there was a period known as the "Dutch Golden Age" where the Netherlands was the cultural leader of Europe.

Although the Dutch Golden Age wasn't quite as philosophical as the European Enlightenment as a whole, Dutch culture was nonetheless a trailblazer for liberty in Europe. Ever since the

Netherlands won its independence from Spain, it has been among the most liberal nations in Europe.

The Netherlands is commonly considered the birthplace of capitalism. Many of the brightest thinkers and ambitious business people immigrated to the Netherlands after the Renaissance because of the degree of liberty given to Dutch citizens and the potential it provided for business ventures.

For quite some time, the Netherlands was the economic leader in Europe because they were the first nation to fully embrace maritime trading.

Russian Enlightenment

The Enlightenment in Russia is interesting because it marks the integration of Russia into European culture, i.e. the "Europeanization" of Russia.

Previously, Russia had been a relatively uneducated nation. This wasn't necessarily a bad thing. There's nothing wrong with being a simple, agricultural society.

However, during the Russian Enlightenment the power elite wanted to significantly improve the educational standing of Russian citizens. That is, they wanted to integrate the educational systems from Western Europe into Russian society. They wanted to bring Russia up to speed, so to speak.

The refreshing thing about Russia's mindset relative to the rest of Europe is that they weren't as fiercely competitive. Most nations during the Enlightenment were hyper-focused on scientific progress and military advancement, but the Russians weren't in a position to be forerunners in those areas.

Instead, the Russian leaders—particularly Catherine II—had more modest goals. They wanted to educate Russian citizens on what it means to be a contributing member of society. In short, they wanted to teach the Russian citizens how to discover a higher purpose in life.

German Enlightenment

Generally the Enlightenment is associated with a very liberal culture, but Germany (known as Prussia at this time) is an interesting example of a culture which took a more conservative approach to educational progress. The Germans definitely embraced Enlightenment values, but they didn't see rational thinking as being incompatible with traditional religion.

Instead, the German Enlightenment produced rational thinkers who explored a wide range of spiritual and metaphysical topics. They weren't quite as focused on scientific materialism as other European countries. If you are interested in occult studies, secret societies, metaphysics, etc., then you will find German history interesting. This is a culture with a deeply metaphysical history.

Another unique characteristic of the German Enlightenment was the relatively low income inequality of their society. In most of the Europe, the power elite controlled the majority of wealth while the rest of society executed daily labor.

However, in Germany a significant portion of the society was considered *middle class* and there was a relatively uninfluential power elite. The large middle class served as a strength for German culture because it eventually developed into a leading academic community. There was a strong national bond which developed in Germany based on the combination of their conservative values and enlightened ideals.

An important movement known as Romanticism started in Germany and spread across all of the Western world (including the USA where it would later inspire transcendentalism). Romanticism was basically a reaction to the hyper-rational culture that had developed in Europe as a result of scientific materialism.

Associated with Gothic culture, Romanticism didn't shy away from dark emotions. There is an emphasis on individual experience and appreciating the full-range of emotions. Things such as heartbreak and depression for male characters became common themes, which was groundbreaking at this point in history.

French Enlightenment

Paris is traditionally referred to as the "cultural capital of

Europe" and the French Enlightenment is why. Ironically, historians don't usually specify a "French Enlightenment" because the European Enlightenment as a whole was centered in France.

Similar to the Netherlands, France was one of the most liberal countries in all of Europe. Oftentimes France and Germany are contrasted in the Enlightenment because France was so radically progressive while Germany preferred a more conservative approach.

However, while the Netherlands was very liberal in terms of economics (capitalism), France was the champion of liberty. That is, the French people demanded a society free of governmental oppression. The economic concept of *laissez-faire* (French for "let go, let it be") originated during this period in France.

Traditionally, aristocratic social life had been centered on the royal court of any given kingdom. However, the culture of France progressed so much during this period that modern forms of socialization started to emerge. More specifically, the upper class in France started to socialize via private parties—known as salons—as opposed to parties in the royal courts.

While Germany was characterized by a burgeoning middle class, France had a more stratified social structure. The social life in France can be described through two archetypes:

1. "polite society" – the most sophisticated members of society who frequented exclusive salons. In order to be a member of this group, you must have been well-versed in all things philosophical and known how to conduct yourself with polished civility.
2. "the bourgeoisie" – also spelled as "boujee" in modern America, this is a pejorative term which basically describes the French citizens who attempted to emulate the lifestyle of the polite society, without possessing the philosophical spirit.

While polite society behaved according to a love for wisdom, the bourgeoisie lacked this philosophical drive. Therefore, they behaved according to more basic desires (i.e. the desire to be perceived as a member of the upper class).

The polite society lived a heavenly life as a result of their philosophical labors, whereas the bourgeoisie were merely trying to project that image in vain.

In other words, the bourgeoisie behaved as if they had achieved material abundance (enlightenment) because it was socially fashionable, but they didn't actually do the introspective work required to attain such abundance.

English Enlightenment

The culture in England was so far ahead of the rest of Europe that the English citizens say they never experienced an "English Enlightenment". Instead, England claims that enlightened ideals successfully became an integral part of English culture during the Renaissance.

In other words, English culture became so civilized during the Renaissance that there was no need to experience an English Enlightenment a century or two later.

At this point in history, England had already become a world superpower. They were global leaders militarily, economically, and intellectually.

Although the Dutch got a head start on the English in the arena of commerce, England would eventually surpass them as the major economic power in the Europe. (London is known as the banking capital of the world.)

This is in large part thanks to the geographic advantages that England had over the rest of Europe. England was the only major power at this time to not be attached to continental Europe. This gave England a lot of freedom and flexibility to conduct maritime trade. In addition, they didn't have to worry about militarily conflicts to the same degree of as most of Europe because of their geographical isolation.

Obviously England has a lot in common with the USA, but geographical isolation in particular has played a key role in foreign policy for both nations. England has generally displayed a preference to develop their culture independently from continental

Europe and stay relatively neutral in foreign affairs—a stance later championed by American George Washington.

10 UNITED STATES OF AMERICA

Great Awakening

America is a nation founded on enlightened ideals, and so there wasn't any sort of enlightenment movement like you saw in Europe. On the contrary, you actually saw the opposite sort of development. In America, people gradually became too rational/materialistic, to the point where they weren't taking religion seriously enough.

Therefore, you had a movement known as the Great Awakening where there was a revival of religion in America.

The ideological dynamics of the Great Awakening were the exact opposite of the ideas promoted by the Enlightenment. You might think this would be considered a step back for society, but the Great Awakening was actually a very positive development.

This movement serves as a great example of what can happen when a group of take an unbalanced approach to growth, i.e. discarding older belief systems entirely when newer, more innovative belief systems are constructed.

When one belief system is stretched too far (rationalism/materialism), a counterbalance movement (Great Awakening) becomes necessary to restore harmonious growth for the society.

Founding Fathers

If we look at the history of the United States in a vacuum—that is, with disregard to anything prior to the American colonies—then we tend to think that the Founding Fathers must have been relatively unsophisticated, compared to modern standards.

Surely with all of the advances in technology since 1776,

our modern decision makers must be wiser today than the Founding Fathers were back then, right?

I want to give you a slightly different perspective.

The birth of the United States of America was the capstone, the crowning achievement, for the entire European Enlightenment.

Above all else, the Enlightenment thinkers wanted to live in a society based on **LIBERTY**—and after centuries of struggle—history shows us that this goal wasn't possible to achieve Europe. Therefore, many European people developed a personal, deeply passionate interest in the founding of the USA.

America was an opportunity to build a culture based on cooperation, as opposed to the warring culture that had been plaguing Europe for so long.

British America

Americans were happy to have their independence. But beyond that, it was unclear how to best proceed.

Many Americans advocated for peaceful and cooperative relations with Britain. There were many benefits to staying closely allied with the British, specifically financially.

London was the leading banking center in the Western world at the time and so friendly relations with Britain would provide greater resources for accelerating the growth of the new American economy.

In terms of foreign policy, the Americans basically had to choose whether to collaborate more with Britain or with France. These two nations were major powers in Europe, and they were bitter rivals. There was a constant tug-of-war between British and French politics in early America.

Although there were many convenient benefits of remaining close allies with Britain, opposing voices feared that Britain would seek to regain control over the colonies if America didn't distance itself enough (and the War of 1812 proved this fear to be valid!).

French America

The British influence on America is obvious, but when you take a deep look at early America you will see that France had an arguably greater influence on American culture.

The American colonies were a direct transplant of British culture. However, the philosophical foundations of America are a mirror image of French values. The French motto during the Enlightenment was "Liberty, Equality, Fraternity".

As discussed last chapter, England's history has been relatively stable since the Renaissance. England didn't need to experience political turmoil during the Enlightenment because progressive ideals were integrated into England during the Renaissance.

On the contrary, France literally had to overthrow their monarchy by force during the French Revolution—maybe the most famous revolution in world history—in order to build a fair society. In other words, French politicians were forced to adopt a radically progressive ideals in order secure individual liberty.

Although France eventually successfully integrated democracy into their country, it was a very slow process. In other words, the cultural acceleration that the French people desired was simply not possible with the longstanding rigidity of European culture. America was important to France because it had to the potential to be the realization of the overarching French dream —a nation of liberty.

While the British-influenced Americans took a more level-headed approach to politics, the French-influenced Americans were intensely liberal. They were deeply apprehensive that a lukewarm approach towards American sovereignty and a reliance on Great Britain would be detrimental to American growth.

Basically, the French-influenced Americans believed that without extreme prudence, America would waste the golden opportunity that is the American experiment. Independence from Britain needed to be taken very seriously and radical policies needed to be implemented in order to prevent America from eventually squandering its independence.

Federalist Party

Now transitioning to early American domestic policy, there were two majors political parties: the Federalists and the Anti-Federalists. The names are pretty self-explanatory. The Federalists favored a strong central government and the Anti-Federalists wanted a minimal central government.

Typically as Americans we think of our federal government as a good thing and, to a large extent, it is a good thing.

However, there is a very wide range of ways to structure your government and in the case of America, the Founding Fathers needed to decide how to best distribute power between the federal government and the states. Here are just a few of the key decisions the Founding Fathers needed to make:

- ☐ **Executive Branch** – How strong should the position of the *president* be?

    Originally, the plan for the United States was to have a group of states that would be similar to the European states in terms of independence and diversity. A strong executive branch would detract from the autonomy of the states.

    In addition, one of the biggest sticking points for the Founding Fathers was to curb the powers of the president so that the position never developed into a kingship. The entire European Enlightenment aimed to decentralize power away from the kings and so the Americans needed to structure the government wisely to ensure that the presidency didn't evolve into a monarchy.

- ☐ **Federal Banking** – Should most money be kept in a centralized *national bank* or in separate *state banks*?

    Banking is something that might not seem like a big deal, but it is actually one of the most critical elements of government. In short, the distribution of finances determines which portions of the economy can grow more rapidly.

Federalists like Alexander Hamilton argued that the majority of funds should be kept in the federal bank so that they could be allocated most effectively. The Federalists wanted to convert all state debts from the Revolutionary War into one national debt. They also wanted establish a protective tariff on foreign trade imports.

- ☐ **Diversity** – Most importantly, distinct and sovereign state governments would facilitate the growth of a diverse American culture.

As previously mentioned, America is supposed to be a nation with the cultural diversity of Europe—but with a much higher degree of cooperation.

Although a strong centralized government is convenient in short term because it ensures stability, the United States of America is not supposed to be a nation built on convenience. Our predecessors from the European Enlightenment devoted their life to advocating for a decentralized power structure.

Federalists were very practically minded and they argued that the benefits of strong centralized government outweighed the weaknesses. They also argued that the power of the government could be held in check with a proper distribution of power (Executive, Legislative, and Judicial).

Anti-Federalist Party

This group, influenced by France and led by Thomas Jefferson, advocated that the federal government should *only* possess the powers that formerly belonged to the English monarchy during the colonial period. All of the other powers should go to the states.

The Anti-Federalists weren't so much opposed to a federal government as they were opposed to limiting the liberty of people in individual states. Choices made by a federal government limit the opportunities for choices by state governments.

Basically, the Federalists and Anti-Federalists were debating this question: should the United States of America be built more so on unity or diversity?

With a strong federal government, the United States as a whole could potentially develop into a leading world economy relatively rapidly (similar to Great Britain).

With an emphasis on distinct state governments, the *individual states* could potentially develop into leading world economies (similar to multiple nations in Europe). When you combine this set of strong state economies with a high degree of interstate cooperation, the United States could potentially build an economy stronger than all of Europe combined.

Articles of Confederation

The first constitution of the United States was more aligned with the Anti-Federalist vision for America.

The Articles of Confederation and Perpetual Union defined the United States as a "league of friends." The idea was to have sovereign, independent states with cooperative relationships—particularly based on trade.

There was a weak central government that was only granted the powers that previously belonged to England. In addition, there was no office of president under the Articles.

However, as time went by, the central government came to the conclusion that they didn't have the necessary power to properly govern the states. In other words, the central government wasn't able to effectively ensure cooperation among the states.

A few key problems with the Articles included:
- inability to organize a national army strong enough to defend America
- no power to tax the states resulted in an extreme shortage of centralized funds
- no federal court to mediate interstate disagreements
- no executive branch to enforce laws passed by congress

U.S. Constitution

Eventually, the early American leaders decided that amendments to the Articles of Confederation could not sufficiently strengthen the central government. Therefore, they completely abandoned the Articles and created the Constitution of the United States.

Here's a few key characteristics of the US Constitution:
- Office of the President
- Dual-chamber congress (Senate and House of Representatives)
- Federal Court system
- Congress has power to draft a military
- Congress regulates trade (domestic and foreign) and sets tariffs
- Federal taxation of the states
- Lighter requirements to pass amendments

The initial phrase of the Constitution, which is written in huge letters is: "WE THE PEOPLE". The overarching vision for the United States is for the people to govern themselves directly. In other words, we are a republic that wants to be as democratic as is realistically possible.

Under the Constitution, the new federal government consisted of three parts: Executive, Legislative, and Judicial. This structure was designed to provide a system of checks-and-balances, where the power of each branch is limited by the other two branches.

With the Bill of Rights, citizens were guaranteed a set of inalienable rights which have completely shaped the history of America.

Strict vs. Loose Interpretation

One of the key debates in American politics involves the distribution of state powers and federal powers. This has been an on-going debate since the beginning of the nation.

The Federalists argued that the federal government should possess all governmental powers that are not explicitly reserved for the states in the Constitution, and their policy is known as loose interpretation.

On the other hand, the Anti-Federalists advocated for strict interpretation, which means that the federal government should only possess the powers that are explicitly mentioned in the Constitution. In other words, strict interpretation gives the States the power to resolve gray areas on their own. If the federal government wants to expand their powers, then they need to do so with the approval of Congress.

Trailblazer for Freedom

Although the American vision is to spread democracy, the American vision is not to spread democracy by *force*. To attempt to override the sovereignty of foreign nations and the free will of their citizens is an arrogant, futile endeavor that has unfortunately been pursued by some American leaders over the course of history.

Rather than spreading democracy by force, we are supposed to utilize our democracy to its fullest potential, thereby setting the standard for all world government to follow. Other countries will be magnetized to our lifestyle and make calls for more democracy to be integrated into their government.

It's a natural progression for humanity to achieve more freedom over time and so we only need to worry about setting a good example. Democracy will be spread around the globe by free-will choices rather than by force.

11 AGE OF AQUARIUS

Greek Words for Time

In ancient Greek culture, they used three different words for time:

- ☐ **Chronos** *(Greek name for Saturn, ruler of Aquarius)*
    - *Quantity of time*: empirical, measures years, days, hours, etc.
    - *Passive time*: everyone experiences it, eventual death
    - Circular time (cyclical), four seasons
    - Used to organize daily life and communicate in terms of spatial time

- ☐ **Kairos**
    - *Quality of time*: energetic signature of a given moment or period of time
    - *Active time*: often refers to moments where action is auspicious, where you must choose to act or participate
    - Loosely translatable to the modern words "opportunity" or "mood"
    - Can describe personal moments or collective experience
    - Very broad potential usage, more subjective than *chronos and aion*

- ☐ **Aion**
    - Complex term that can refer to a few different things

- *Eternity* - cosmic time, boundless, infinite
- *Eon* - long periods of earthly time
- *Generations* - Golden Age, Silver Age, Age of Aquarius, etc.
- Movement of astrological bodies, solar system is built like a clock

NOTE: Some scholars argue that *aion* refers to cyclical time, rather than *chronos*. *Aion* is the void from which *chronos* emerged. *Chronos* describes the cycles of time characteristic of the Fall of Man (birth to death, four seasons) and *Aion* can describe prolonged, heavenly cycles of time.

Astronomy

From a purely astronomical perspective, the existence of the Age of Aquarius is not debatable. It's a period of time based on the physical movement of our planet through space.

In short, the 12 zodiac signs form a circle in the sky around Earth, like the 12 numbers on a clock. Earth moves through the full cycle roughly every 24,000 years and we are currently on the borderline between **Pisces** and **Aquarius**.

Most modern scholars consider the Age of Aquarius to only be a unit of time and reject the notion that it has any sort of relationship with the collective human experience.

For more info on the astronomical basis, you can research the precession of the equinox.

Logos

Astrology—and any other discipline ending in "-*logy*"—is intrinsically connected with the Greek word *logos* (as in ethos, pathos, logos). The suffix *–logy* basically means "science or systematic discourse based upon *logos*".

Logos is commonly translated into English as "Word", as in John 1:1

> "In the beginning was the Word, and the Word was with God, and the Word was God."

However, *logos* is one of the most complex words in Western culture and therefore the term "word" doesn't sufficiently explain it. Some of the other modern words used to describe *logos* include: "logic", "purpose", "plan", "structure", "thought", among others.

In secular education, *logos* is essentially a synonym for "logic".

While there is definitely a connection between *logos* and logic, the philosophy underlying *logos* goes much deeper than our modern notion of logic.

The concept of *logos* can be explored in countless ways but, from a spiritual perspective, it basically refers to the overarching plan for our entire cycle of creation. *Logos* is the blueprint that God had in mind while constructing our material reality. It describes God's plan for the steady evolution of mankind

Astrology

When we look at the roots of the term *astrology,* you can say that astrology refers to the description of *logos* using the heavenly bodies.

- *astron* (Greek for "heavenly bodies")
- *-logia* (Greek for "science of the Logos")

In other words, astrology is the use of the heavenly bodies to describe God's plan for earth, on both individual and collective levels.

So when describing the Age of Aquarius in terms of astrology, it is a period of time that was planned by God. To some extent, there are certain energetic characteristics that will be more pronounced on earth during the Age of Aquarius.

Astronomy helps us think of the Age of Aquarius in terms of *chronos*. That is, it's a period of time that can be physically observed and it is certain to arrive.

On the other hand, astrology helps us understand the Age of Aquarius in terms of *kairos* and *aion.*

Relative to *kairos*, the Age of Aquarius will be charged with Aquarian energy and Aquarian pursuits are likely to succeed. It will be a Golden Age because of the energetic signature of abundance on earth.

Relative to *aion*, the Age of Aquarius is a cosmically planned period of time. It is one of a number of astrological ages that has been experienced on earth. It will be a Golden Age because it is governed by Saturn.

Saturn and Uranus

I prefer to use the 7 classical planets (Sun, Moon, Mercury, Venus, Mars, Jupiter, Saturn) when discussing astrology because of the simplicity and symmetry that they provide. However, the planet Uranus is the co-ruler of Aquarius alongside Saturn in modern astrology.

The name "Uranus" comes from the Greek word for heavens: *ouranos*. This is a word for heavens that is commonly used in the New Testament (which was originally written in Greek).

Ouranos is also a primordial spirit in Greek mythology that is associated with the sky, the heavens, and infinity. Ouranos is the father of the Titans, and therefore Saturn.

When considering the sign of Aquarius, you can say that it is ruled by the partnership of Saturn and the heavens (Uranus).

Upon first consideration, it might seem paradoxical to have a sign ruled by Saturn and Uranus because they are generally characterized as polar opposites (Saturn as traditional, Uranus as revolutionary).

However, the energies of Uranus actually serve to illuminate the Aquarian nature that also exists in Saturn. Astrologically speaking, Saturn is the most complex planet in our solar system and it is equally at home in both Capricorn and Aquarius. In other words, if you only think of Saturn in terms of Capricorn energy, then you have not acquired a holistic understanding of Saturn.

Water-Bearer

The Hebrew word *shamayim* refers to the heavens in the Old Testament, and it can give us interesting insights into the nature of Aquarius.

Shamayim is commonly translated into English as "sky", but if you break it down you see that *shamayim* comes from two other Hebrew words:
- *sham* ("lofty place" or more loosely "mountaintop")
- *mayim* (literally "water")

Thus, the Hebrew word for heavens basically means "water from up high" or "where the rain comes from". *Shamayim* sends water to the earth so that life can grow (water + earth = life).

~~~~~~

The first symbol associated with Aquarius is the **Water-Bearer**. This symbol depicts Aquarius as a man pouring out a jug of water.

You can also symbolize Aquarius as a woman pouring water, but a man is typically used because Aquarius is a masculine sign.

On a mundane level, the Water-Bearer is a symbol for AGRICULTURE ! Man puts a seed into the earth and adds water, and with time we get a harvest.

You take limited natural resources (earth, water, time) and you literally multiply them to produce an ABUNDANCE of highly valuable natural resources (vegetables, fruits, trees).

On a metaphysical level, it goes deeper. The Water-Bearer symbolizes man bringing heaven to earth.

The heavens (*shamayim*) are where water pours down from the mountaintop, and the Water-Bearer does that same thing amongst the people on earth. The Water-Bearer illustrates one of the central characteristics of the Aquarian archetype: humanitarianism, or humble service to reduce human suffering on earth.

Air Waves

The other major symbol for Aquarius—also called the glyph—is the Air Waves.

Aquarius is an AIR sign and *not* a water sign. Yes, this is ironic considering that the word "aqua" is in the name and its major symbol is a Water-Bearer.

Nonetheless, the air element is a much more accurate descriptor of the Aquarian archetype than water. Whereas water signs are highly emotional and intuitive, air signs are intellectual and highly idealistic.

The Aquarian intellect isn't to be compared to the average human intellect. The Aquarian mind is very broad, and even a bit psychic. While modern society uses the intellect to examine the world through scientific materialism, an Aquarian uses the intellect to examine the world through broad spiritual paradigms.

The Air Waves symbolize the transfer of information through the air. In other words, the Air Waves illustrate the favorite pastime of Aquarius: sharing new ideas!

Transcendentalism

Another defining characteristic of Aquarius is the burning desire for freedom.

This desire for liberty is so intense that Aquarius has commonly been described as rebellious. That is, rebelling against social norms to express their individuality. The word "rebellious" isn't necessarily inaccurate, but it is potentially misleading.

Traditionally, rebellion has been the word used to describe the actions of the fallen angels. Religion tells us that the fallen angels contested that they knew better than God, and therefore they willingly behaved in a way that was counterproductive to God's plan for earth. The fallen angels rebelled against God.

Now, you can definitely say that Aquarius does rebel against *human power structures*. That is, Aquarius tends to behave in a way that can disturb the status quo. Human power structures have a tendency to become stagnant over time and oftentimes an Aquarian shock of electricity causes a stir.

But to say that Aquarius is inherently opposed to divine tradition, to say that Aquarius rebels against God? This idea is completely out of touch with the reality of Aquarius!

Let us not forget that Aquarius is literally ruled by the planet of tradition: Saturn.

A much more accurate descriptor of Aquarius is *transcendent*, rather than rebellious. Aquarius helps humanity transcend self-limiting belief patterns. This does not mean that tradition is discarded, but rather that tradition is refreshed.

Avant-Garde

During the French Enlightenment there was a popular archetype known as the "avant-garde". Traditionally, the avant-garde is a group of people who publicly lead whatever contemporary cultural advancements are fashionable.

In my opinion, this is a pejorative term that was used to describe people in France who used Enlightenment principles in vain.

The avante-garde do generally possess above-average intelligence, but they also act with a sense of pride that is unbecoming of true philosophers. They're usually ambitious and eager to receive public recognition for their contributions to society.

Understandably, people have a tendency to describe Aquarians as avant-garde because it is a revolutionary sign and Aquarians tend to be at the cutting-edge of technology.

Personally, I don't think avant-garde is an accurate descriptor of Aquarius because it is off-base from the proper Aquarian mindset. The avant-garde practice humanitarianism from an ego-centric perspective while Aquarians practice humanitarianism from a perspective of divine service.

Aquarius does not lead social evolution, so to speak, but rather Aquarius refreshes tradition. There's a subtle distinction to be made there.

USA in Aquarius

The United States is the trailblazer for freedom, the trailblazer for democracy, and the trailblazer for Aquarian consciousness.

Here's the Aquarian plan for the USA:

Division → Unity → Diversity

What this progression shows is that diversity is not possible without unity. The Aquarian plan for the USA—and for earth—is increased diversity.

Tragically, the United States has actually regressed as of late. We went from "One Nation Under God" to a nation filled with internal divisions. This is certainly problematic, and it is an obstacle that the USA must overcome in order to manifest Aquarian levels of diversity.

In practical terms, the Aquarian vision for the United States is to have the diversity of Europe with a much higher degree of cooperation between states. In the USA, each individual state can and should become a self-sufficient economy. Global and domestic trade is good thing, but economic self-sufficiency is the primary focus.

There should not be any sort of chronic fear among the people that their basic fundamental needs cannot be met due to a lack of natural resources. The idea that we do not have enough natural resources in America—or on earth—is simply not a reality.

The United States is not overpopulated. Maybe a little too urbanized, but there is still plenty of resources. And even if some people do think that our planet has scarcity of natural resources, then we can always multiply our natural resources through agriculture to meet all of our basic needs in abundance.

Aquarian Technology

Aquarius is commonly referred to as the sign of technology.

The word *technology* can be broken down into the following roots:

- *tekhne* (Greek for "art, craft, systematic discourse")
  - *teks-* (Proto-Indo-European for "to weave")
- *–logia* (Greek for "science relating to *logos*")

Here we see that the word technology loosely translates to "art created according to *logos*" or "weaving combined with *logos*".

It's tough to explain the significance of weaving in only a few words, but basically weaving is one of the best metaphors to describe the process of karmically constructing your own reality. In other words, you *weave* together multiple streams of your individual consciousness in order to manifest your experience.

This is an advanced spiritual concept, but it needs to be discussed in order to properly communicate what technology means to Aquarius. Aquarian technology is the systematic, artistic weaving of your consciousness in order to manifest a desired experience (in harmony with *logos*).

This is obviously in sharp contrast to modern notions of "technology". Modern technology generally refers to machinery.

While a machine is indeed a form of technology, they are actually a relatively primitive form of technology. A machine basically transforms a human input into a desired output through a mechanical process. A machine is inorganic.

Higher forms of technology are organic, creative processes. That is, advanced technology does not produce the desired output mechanically. Higher forms of technology require active choices from people in order to manifest the desired output.

Aquarian technology refers to creative processes, not a mechanical ones. The word "techniques" is a better descriptor of Aquarian technology than the modern materialistic concepts of what technology is.

It's worth mentioning that the root *"teks-"* isn't limited to the word technique and technology. *"Teks-"* actually gives us a number of other words including: "text", "technical", "architect", and Greek *"tekton"* (the word used to describe Jesus and Joseph as "carpenters" in the New Testament).

Aquarian Business Models

In the Age of Information, naturally the most powerful business products will be ideas. Here's a few things to consider about the business environment in the Aquarian Age:

☐ Time and Money

For many generations the earth has been dominated by patriarchal societies. By and large, men have traditionally made the majority of microeconomic decisions within the family. In other words, the global economy was historically built around men spending money.

In the Digital Age, this dynamic is becoming increasingly outdated. The most valuable currency in the Aquarian Age is the consumer's mental energy, or simply their TIME.

Assuming that access to digital technology isn't a problem, <u>all members of society have equal value to businesses</u> in the Aquarian Age because all people have the same amount of time.

It's no longer a matter of "How do we get the consumer's money?" but rather "How do we attract the consumer's attention?"

☐ Cooperation First, Competition Second

In the Western hemisphere, there has long been a generally accepted set of social ethics for individual behavior. For a period of time, businesses went unchecked by these ethical standards as capitalism exploded in popularity.

This dynamic is already eroding in the USA, where consumers have started demanding social responsibility from corporations.

In the Aquarian Age, an ethical standard will crystallize in the business arena so that individuals will not even attempt to build a business unethically. This is not for fear of punishment, but rather because such business models will clearly be uncompetitive and unsustainable in Aquarian markets.

☐ **Harvesting of Souls**

The most basic principle of marketing is to provide the consumer with value. That is, your business should improve the life of the consumer.

This is a dynamic that will be expanded to the fullest extent in the Aquarian Age. All success in the business arena will be directly proportional to the amount of value provided to consumers, particularly with respect to limited time constraints.

Vapid forms of entertainment will wane in popularity as consumers will simply have many more productive and rewarding ways to spend their time.

Building a sustainable business will be an organic process where the business sells a product to a consumer and—after a period of time—the consumer reaps benefits from the product.

This is a win-win situation, where the business is able to sell a product and the consumer is able to genuinely improve their quality of life through the product. Customer loyalty will be built organically as the consumers will naturally be attracted back to businesses who improved their lives in the past.

Pisces to Aquarius

A common question within spiritual circles is: "When will we officially move from the Age of Pisces to the Age of Aquarius?"

Pisces and Aquarius are two different forms of consciousness, and each individual makes the choice to move from Piscean paradigms to Aquarian paradigms at their own pace.

You could say that the Age of Aquarius officially begins when the majority of humanity embraces the Aquarian consciousness. However, the chronological date that this occurs is not significant.

It's worth knowing that you can not progress to the Aquarian consciousness without first mastering the Piscean consciousness. The Piscean consciousness is based around unity and the Aquarian consciousness is based around diversity. There is no diversity without unity.

12 END OF TIME

Time Bubble

As discussed previously, the human concept of time is really just a circular bubble of time, so to speak, that was created by human choices. During the original Golden Age, our planet existed in perfect harmony with the rest of the universe and time was infinite—no beginning and no end.

When the planet was lowered in vibration through the Fall of Man, the humans who embodied on earth gradually forgot about their divine heritage. Eventually, humans collectively came to the conclusion that this physical reality is the *only* reality, and thus our separate bubble of time was created.

The End of Time is the completion of the circle between the original Golden Age and the dawning Golden Age of Aquarius. And so the End of Time is simply the reunification of earth with the rest of the cosmos.

End of Chronos

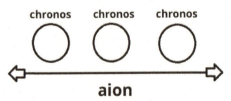

Drawing upon the Greek concepts of time discussed last chapter, we can more accurately frame the End of Time as the End of *Chronos*. And with the End of chronos, the planet will return to the infinite, cosmic timeline of Aion.

Chronos is a member of the divine family tree described in

Greek mythology, but it is most important to understand the symbolism behind Chronos.

Of course, the name Chronos literally means "time", but a more precise description of Chronos is "human time". That is, Chronos represents the sense of time that humans have experienced on earth since the Fall of Man. You could say that since the Fall of Man, humans have been collectively trapped in the experience of Chronos.

This experience of Chronos gave rise to common notions such as "the beginning of time", "the end of time", "past, present, and future", and "death". All of these concepts don't exist from a cosmic perspective, but rather were created from limited frames of understanding on earth.

Chronic Disease

In practical terms, when humans are trapped inside of Chronos their default experience is suffering. In other words, their lives are plagued by *chronic* health issues.

We refer to permanent diseases as chronic because they follow you to your death. Chronic diseases always shorten your lifespan and there is no mechanical cure for them.

When you transcend Chronos, your lifespan is not artificially shortened by chronic disease—or simply chronic stress. Instead of suffering, your experience on earth is characterized by blissful creativity.

That's not to say that your life on the physical plane is literally infinite once you transcend Chronos. It's a natural part of physical reality to experience a finite lifespan. It allows you to experiment with different choices in different lifetimes, and therefore gain a diverse set of experiences.

However, the human concept of "death" is far removed from the spiritual experience of exiting the physical plane. From a spiritual perspective, you don't experience the fear-based emotions associated with human death because you know that you are simply returning to the spiritual realm.

Crystallization

For the most part, Western culture has been built upon Judeo-Christian values.

A few of these include, but are not limited to:

- ☐ equality of all people under God (men, women, and children)
- ☐ respect for human dignity
- ☐ respect for the elderly
- ☐ charity
- ☐ legal system available to all members of society
- ☐ animal rights

These are universal principles that we consider normal parts of life in the USA, but before Judaism they were absent from human culture. In the Golden Age, these are the type of values that will crystallize into the global culture because they benefit all people.

However, I want to make it very clear that—although there will be a universally-shared set of moral values—that does not mean that all cultures on earth must be or will be homogeneous.

On the contrary, the most dominant value of all will be the appreciation of diversity.

It might seem like a unity of values would limit the diversity on earth, but ironically the unity of values actually increases the diversity on earth. Universal morality will prevent reckless, self-destructive behaviors and therefore more time and energy will be available for individuals to exercise their creativity. Naturally, this increase in creativity will yield an increase in cultural diversity.

Light Quotient

$$\frac{\sum \text{thoughts, words, behaviors}}{\text{will of God}}$$

Another way to frame the End of Time is by using the concept of a light quotient. I discuss light quotients. Basically, a light quotient is the proportion to which an individual's aura is in harmony with the will of God, or *logos*.

In other words, an individual's light quotient is the extent to which their karma (sum of choices over time) aligns with the original divine plan for creation.

(NOTE: *Greek Σ is the mathematical symbol for summation, or addition of all parts*)

Furthermore, the *collective* light quotient on earth is always the sum of all individual light quotients.

During a Golden Age, the choices made by individuals are fully aligned with the will of God. Again, this is NOT because the individuals fear punishment from God, but rather because the individuals understand that aligning themselves with God is in their own enlightened self-interest, i.e. it's optimal.

As previously mentioned, there have been a number of minor Golden Ages over the course of history where a significant amount of light has been anchored to the earth. For example, for the first few centuries after the life of Jesus there was a significant number of believers who experienced enlightenment. And obviously, the entire idea of the European Enlightenment is that the light quotient of Europe was increasing during that time.

However, the reason I refer to these types of time periods as "minor" Golden Ages is because they gradually faded away over time. That is, the mental framework that sparks a minor Golden Age isn't able to be flawlessly passed down through multiple generations due to the historical limitations of communication.

Prior to the internet, there were two major ways to pass down wisdom over time:
1) Word of mouth
2) Written texts (by hand for most of history, printed since the Renaissance.)

It's not like these methods are completely ineffective, but they are also not perfect for a number of reasons. The original message was always distorted over time, historically speaking.

Universal Library

Our planet is just totally different since the creation of the internet.

We commonly compare the internet to preceding technologies, namely radio and television. And this is for good reason. In the context of things like daily news distribution or business marketing, the internet is a more efficient distribution channel than radio and television.

However, if you only think of the internet as a better version of radio and TV, then you miss the bigger picture.

The internet is basically a combination of all of the libraries in the world. The value of the internet completely dwarfs the value of any individual library.

Before the internet, libraries were the only place you could go to access a universal set of information. In other words, if you wanted to learn about any subject in depth—history, philosophy, mathematics, physics, chemistry, etc.—then you needed to go to a library. (Or if you had enough resources, attend a university).

So it's safe to say that the access to information was increased tremendously with the internet. Not only are all of the world's libraries combined into one, but they are also accessible from virtually anywhere on the planet, INSTANTLY!

Furthermore, only a fraction of the world's population actually contributed to the information systems contained in traditional libraries. In other words, most people never wrote books and therefore they didn't contribute to libraries.

And with radio and television, the information distribution was still relatively centralized. Corporations and the government basically had control over the mass distribution of information.

With the internet, the global information system receives input from the majority of the population (at least in developed nations, like the USA). And this occurs on an instantaneous basis, i.e. whenever people feel like posting on the internet, they can do it immediately.

This is so radically different from most history, where the average person could only contribute to the global information system via physical word of mouth.

One of the most exciting implications of the internet is that it provides a platform for the steady advancement of human culture. Once wisdom is accepted and integrated into society, we won't forget it.

Whereas historically the wisdom of a minor Golden Age always faded out of the collective consciousness, the wisdom will be permanently engraved into the collective consciousness with the internet in the Age of Aquarius.

Eschatology

The End of Time is a concept that is discussed in all religions, as I'm sure you're already aware of. The term used to describe the End of Time in religion is "eschatology", which comes from Greek roots *eskhatos* ("final, last") and *logia* ("relating to *logos*"). Thus, eschatology refers to the final part of the divine plan for creation.

- Popular eschatological texts, such as the Book of Revelation, were written from a limited state of consciousness. That is, they are not perfect descriptions of the End of Time. And truly, no text is a perfect description of the End of Time. But that is especially true for texts that were written such a long time ago.

- Most eschatological texts were written from a fear-based state of consciousness. They can easily give people the idea that the End of Time is something to fear. It is indeed important to be prudent about the End of Time, but it's not something you should constantly worry about, per se.

  If you have been genuinely following the word of God, then the End of Time is actually more like an enjoyable harvest, rather than a frightening apocalypse.

- Most eschatological texts were written with a high degree

of flair. In other words, they contain a lot of symbolism. They are not to be interpreted with the linear, analytical mind. They are intended to stretch your imagination.

Free Will Planet

Another commonly held belief that the End of Time will coincide with some sort of miraculous physical manifestation where the entire world will be forced to accept the reality of God.

Some people believe that Jesus will literally descend from the earth while riding on a cloud. Other people believe our ancestors will literally rise from their graves like zombies. And the list goes on.

The entire purpose of our physical reality is to allow individuals to grow in self-awareness through their own free will choices. There must to be some sort of plausible deniability from the perspective of humans. In other words, if individuals chose to deny the reality of God, then God will always respect that choice.

These individuals will be allowed to hold this belief for as long as they choose and God will not force them out of that state of consciousness.

For heaven to send some sort of undeniable manifestation to the entire planet would be totally counterproductive to the spiritual growth of individuals. It would defeat the entire purpose of this physical reality, namely to provide individuals an opportunity to choose to reunite with God.

Age of Capricorn

After the Age of Aquarius, we are scheduled to experience the Age of Capricorn, the age of the goat. You might be wondering, "What will life be like in the Age of Capricorn?"

- ☐ On one hand, there is no guarantee that the End of Time will actually manifest during the Age of Aquarius. It is technically possible that the planet won't manifest a high enough light quotient during the Aquarian Age to say we've actually reached the End of Time. It really just depends on the choices the people make on earth.

In this case, our planet won't look much different than it does now. People will still be trapped in the dualistic struggle of suffering and we will still be awaiting the End of Time.

☐ On the other hand, it's possible that the spiritual growth on the planet continues to accelerate so fast that we don't actually make it 2000 more years to the Age of Capricorn (in a good way). In other words, the planet will progress to the point where all of the lifestreams move on to new creations outside of the current cycle of creation on this planet.

In this case, our planet will basically be a heavenly sphere for individuals to interact on. Life won't be like it is today. There will be no chronic conflict and individuals will be focused purely on new creations.

ABOUT THE AUTHOR

Sean Kayvon Sedghi

Location: Tennessee, USA
Favorite color: green, purple
Favorite animal: goats
Favorite books: Ecclesiastes, Chronicles
Favorite planet: Saturn
Favoirte time in history: right now!

Made in the USA
Monee, IL
04 January 2022